AF574726

An obstetric tragedy

FRONTISPIECE. Princess Charlotte Augusta in the autumn of 1817, shortly before her confinement. By Sir Thomas Lawrence, P.R.A. (Royal Castle of Laeken; Collections Royales de Belgique, Copyright A.C.L., Brussels) [1].

An obstetric tragedy

The case of Her Royal Highness The Princess Charlotte Augusta

Some unpublished documents of 1817

BY FRANCO CRAINZ

Professor of Obstetrics and Gynaecology
University of Rome

William Heinemann Medical Books Ltd
LONDON

First published 1977

ISBN 0 433 06664 4

Printed in Great Britain at the Alden Press, Oxford

Contents

	Introduction	1
I	Princess Charlotte to Sir Richard Croft	4
II	Sir Richard Croft's appointment	10
III	Pregnancy, labour and death	11
IV	Twelve letters, 8–28 November 1817	22
V	Princess Charlotte to Dr Matthew Baillie	31
VI	Count Münster to the Duke of Cambridge	32
VII	Mrs Baillie's notebook	34
	Other documents	43
	Books and pamphlets 1817–1818	48
	Notes	62
	Acknowledgements	76

Plates

	Princess Charlotte Augusta	*frontispiece*
I	Sir Richard Croft in his coffin	*facing page* 2
II	One of Princess Charlotte's letters	*following page* 8
III	One page of the 'Doctors' Report'	*facing page* 72

Introduction

Princess Charlotte Augusta [2] was born at Carlton House, Pall Mall, on 7 January 1796, the only child of George, Prince of Wales, by his consort and first cousin [3] Caroline of Brunswick-Wolfenbüttel.

On 2 May 1816 Princess Charlotte married Prince Leopold of Saxe-Coburg-Saalfeld. She became pregnant in January 1817 and decided to have her child at her own residence, Claremont House, near Esher, Surrey.

The labour began at 7 p.m. on Monday, 3 November 1817, and lasted more than two nights and two days. The unfortunate Princess gave birth to a still-born son at 9 p.m. on Wednesday the 5th and died five and a half hours later, at 2.30 a.m. on Thursday the 6th, two months before her 22nd birthday.

Three doctors had been in attendance: Matthew Baillie [4], her Physician-in-Ordinary, Sir Richard Croft, Bart. [5], her Accoucheur and Surgeon-in-Ordinary, and a Consultant Accoucheur, John Sims [6]. Although completely blameless (the management of the labour had been quite in accordance with the best contemporary practice) Sir Richard Croft shot himself three months later, on 13 February 1818.

King George III had had fifteen children, but Princess Charlotte was his only legitimate grandchild. At her death the direct line of succession was broken.

One of Princess Charlotte's aunts and three of her uncles were married a few months after her death, in the period April to July 1818: Princess Elizabeth to Frederick VI, Landgrave of Hesse-Homburg; Adolphus, Duke of Cambridge, to Princess Augusta of Hesse-Cassel; Edward, Duke of Kent, to Princess Victoria of Saxe-Coburg-Saalfeld, sister of Prince Leopold; William, Duke of Clarence, to Princess Adelaide of Saxe-Meiningen.

Princess Charlotte Augusta, daughter of the Duke of Clarence, was born prematurely on 21 March 1819 and died on the same day. Prince George, son of the Duke of Cambridge, was born on 26 March; Princess Alexandrina Victoria, daughter of the Duke of Kent, on 24 May; Prince George, son of the Duke of Cumberland, on 27 May of the same year. (The Duke of Cumberland had married Princess Frederica of Mecklenburg-Strelitz in 1815 and had had a still-born daughter by her on 27 January 1817.)

The Duke of Kent died on 23 January and King George III on 29 January 1820. The Prince Regent became King George IV and on his death (26 June 1830) was succeeded by the Duke of Clarence, King George III's third son, who became King William IV. (The second son, the Duke of York, had died without issue on 5 January 1827.) King William IV died on 20 June 1837, without issue; the Duchess of Clarence had had a second premature birth (Princess Elizabeth survived only three months, from 10 December 1820 to 4 March 1821) and at least two miscarriages (in September 1819 and in April 1822, the second one being of twins). The crown of Great Britain and Ireland devolved therefore on Princess Alexandrina Victoria, only child of the Duke of Kent, King George III's fourth son. The fifth son, the Duke of Cumberland, became King of Hanover and Duke of Brunswick-Lüneburg in accordance with the Salic Law.

On her accession to the throne Princess Alexandrina Victoria dropped her first name and became Queen Victoria. If the confinement of Princess Charlotte had had a favourable outcome, possibly Princess Alexandrina Victoria would not have been conceived.

In 1831 Prince Leopold became Leopold I, King of the Belgians. Besides being Queen Victoria's maternal uncle he was also the paternal uncle of Prince Albert of Saxe-Coburg-Gotha, the Prince Consort.

* * *

The story of Princess Charlotte's confinement was brilliantly

PLATE I. Sir Richard Croft in his coffin. By Sir Thomas Lawrence, P.R.A. (Property of R. Page Croft Esq., of The Round House, Ware, Herts.) [7].

told by Sir Eardley Holland, F.R.C.S., F.R.C.P., F.R.C.O.G., in his William Meredith Fletcher Shaw Memorial Lecture delivered at the Royal College of Obstetricians and Gynaecologists on 28 September 1951. He had been given access to a series of documents recently discovered at Fanhams Hall, Ware, Herts., where some descendants of Sir Richard Croft through his youngest son, the Rev. Richard, were living. Sir Eardley's paper [8], however, includes only the transcription of some excerpts.

These documents are printed here in full under headings I, II, III and IV. They are followed (V, VI and VII) by three more unpublished documents which have been made available to me over the past years.

In the transcriptions the original spelling has been retained, apart from a few obvious mistakes, and so have the punctuation and the use of capital and small letters. For easier reference the division into paragraphs has sometimes been changed. Where the text had been corrected the final form is given, but the original words or phrases are added as a note if the modification was substantial.

I

Princess Charlotte to Sir Richard Croft

Nine letters written to Sir Richard Croft by Princess Charlotte during her pregnancy

Property of R. Page Croft Esq.,
of The Round House, Ware, Herts.

These are not all the letters sent by the Princess to Sir Richard. When they were found, they were secured by a paper band bearing the endorsement 'Some of these have been destroyed' followed by the initials of the two executors of Sir Richard's will, Matthew Baillie and Thomas Denman [9] (Holland, p. 912) [8].

Except for the day of the week, which she never forgot, the Princess did not date any of these letters; four are dated in a different hand, and one can be dated from internal evidence. These five letters have been placed in chronological order and are followed by the other four.

1

Friday Clermont 14 March
received at *7 PM*[1]

I feel Sure You Will be As glad to hear from me As I am to be able to tell You that the 2^{d} *period* is now *Safely past over A Week* [10].

The Sickness Continues, but has been *greater* than these last 2 days, when I have been troubled With *pains* & irritation like the Nerves of the *lower part* of My *Stomach*, & *Round* the *Navel*.

[1] '14 March / received at *7 PM*' is written in pencil in a different hand.

when first I make Water in the Mg early I do it *Without difficulty*, but it gives me *pain*, & then leaves for a few Minutes after, the *pains below*, which I have already mentioned –

Wind I have been troubled With Within these last 2 days also when I took Your draught prescribed wh: agreed perfectly – Pains in My breasts have Also been frequent lately. The Sickness has been constantly attended With Retching, & at night going to bed 3 alternate days I brought up Everything On my Stomach – these last days I have been *qualmish* like Sea Sick but nothing more As the irritation I have mentioned has chiefly plagued me As it affects me leg & legs With pain Sometimes for a few minutes my back but Seldom –

I Would beg of You to Write to me As Soon As You can Assess the contents of this letter –

C

Since this has been written H.R.H. has been very sick again before breakfast but brought nothing up, except Water[1]

Endorsed: 'Sir Richd Croft' and '7th'

2

Thursday Clermont 9 July 1817[2]

My cold is going off but by no means Yet gone, As it flies about one day in my head, then on my chest, Sometimes like Rheumatismn in my limbs. I have no fever & my Bowels are open & Regular –

Yesterday between 5 & 6 I was overcome With a sort of faintness & Sickness the former went off soon but the latter continued on during the whole of dinner time till afterwards when it quite subsided. of course I had little or no appetite & eat little. I Was not Sick to throw up. To day since breakfast I have begun to feel again Some Sickness but no faintness & nothing so strong As Yesterday.

1 This sentence is written in darker ink in a third hand.

2 '9 July 1817' is written in a different hand. This date was a Wednesday.

This Morning I blew out of my nose A good deal of coagulated blood but my nose did not bleed –

Pray Write to me.

C

3

Sunday Night *Clermont* [10 August][1]

We wish to know if You Will give me leave to go over to Richmond on Tuesday Mg: to a Breakfast at Lady Cardigans [11], in order to See the Regent as it is his Birthday. the distance is but 5 miles, & We Should simply pay our duty & instantly Return home, So that the fatigue I should not think Would be great, as we intend only Staying a Quarter or half an Hour – at the Same time if You think I had *better* give it up, I *Shall* –

Pray Answer me by Return of Post – I Am certainly Much the better for the bleeding.

C

4

Thursday Clermont Augst 15 1817[2]

I am sure You Will be glad to hear I am *not the worse* for the exertion I made on Tuesday, & that I only experienced a little fatigue tho' I Remained but a very short time –

I May As Well See Griffiths [12] on her Return from Woborne, it will be quite time Enough as I have not Anything Very particular to Say to her – I have Seen Mrs Jans [12] & her children, I like their healthy looks amasingly, but it does not Strike me that She appears to be Very Strong, or to be by Any means As far advanced As She Says. However I am probably Wrong as I know little of the matter & You Are A Much better judge –

Pray let me know when Griffiths is to come down –

[1] The Prince Regent's birthday was 12 August.

[2] 'Augst 15 1817' is written in lighter ink in a different hand. This date was a Friday.

5

Friday *Clermont* 29 Aug^{t}[1]

We have Seen Mrs Winchester [12] & like her Appearance, but the question now is, before we finally engage her, what conditions She would come upon, & we Must therefore trouble You to ascertain & let us know this –

I have been teazed only the last 3 days more or less, With Some pain which I conceive to be wind, for which I took the draught You prescribed Some time ago, but I do not think it was of much use – To day as Yet I have had but little windy pains, but altogether I do not feel easy tho' I am not heated, & have no headache –

I shall be glad to hear from you, but do not Wish to trouble You to come down –

6

Saturday Night Clermont

I think it Right to trouble You With a few lines to satisfy the Prince As Well as Myself by hearing Your opinion & advice As to a pale Yellow Sort of discharge that comes on Every Now & then, more or less at times, but Never in Any degree or Quantity Without Any previous posible fatigue or exertion – Also An occasional Sore Sensation in My Stomach & when I breath or Stretch myself up –

I Will only beg of You to Write to me immediately –

Endorsed: 'H R H P. C.' and, upside down, 'Princess'

7

Friday Claremont

If You could ride down here tomorrow I should be Very glad to see You. I do not propose to day As this can only

[1] '29 Aug^{t}' is written in darker ink in a different hand.

Reach You late & if You Came off in consequence of a Summons from me it Would be talked of & make a fuss –

Till *now* I have been As Well As possible daily laying out on the Sopha in the open Air & persuing that Careful quiet plan w^h^ I Wrote You Word of – I have not deserved therefore by Any imprudence on My part that there should be A *Show* of *fresh Blood* wh. has this Mg. occur'd attended too With pain in My legs back & lower Stomach – I felt the pain last night for w^h^ I took My 10 drops of Laudanum. I have Repeated it this Mg more I cannot do –

I confess to some little agitation Yesterday Eg. & to having Sat up on My Sopha Writing A good deal but this is all I can tell You – There is as Yet no quantity of Blood of course therefore I have not put on Any additional clothing but it is *quite fresh* not like the former discharges at different times –

Will You favor me With An Answer by Return of the Servant –

Believing me to be
Ever Your Sincere friend
Charlotte

8

Monday Claremont

I am Very happy to be able to assure You that I Reached this on Saturday Quite safely & Well, & that I have been better ever Since I came. I felt Some pain in the carriage & after I got out, but I attribute it to Gravel, As A great deal has come Away, & continues to do so whenever I feel pain. There has not been Any Appearance at all of other things.

I have been laying all the day on A Sopha out in the Air & enjoyed it excessively. I attempted to Walk a Very little & Slowly for which I do not feel at all the Worse at the time I Was only a little tired wh. is to be Accounted easily for not having used my legs hardly at all for So long a time –

I fear it Will be out of my power to take the Magnesium but Wish Very Much You could Recommend me Anything

PLATE II*a*. One of the letters (I,9) written to Sir Richard Croft by Princess Charlotte Augusta during her pregnancy (Property of R. Page Croft Esq., of The Round House, Ware, Herts.).

visits Vienna & that
I shall be in a better
state of health than
I have been in a great
while — The Prince
makes me in very good
order & address as
nearly to Emm [illegible]
far as possible —
as I had nothing
particular to say further
than what I have
now communicated
to Emm I should not
delay Emm to communi-
cate to see me —
whatever occurs
Emm shall instantly
know —
Believe me [illegible]

PLATE II*b*

PLATE II*c*

else that Would have the Same effect, As I Really think I should be quite free of all pain in my back could I get rid of this complaint – I intend trying to leave off my red draught for a few days in hopes Soon of being able to do quite without it –

Would you be So good As to write to Mrs Louis

The last line of the second page ends with 'Mrs Louis' without any punctuation mark. Possibly one or more further pages are missing. Mrs. Louisa Louis had been the Princess's dresser for many years.

9

Saturday Clermont

I am Sure You Will be glad to hear A good Account of me from Myself. Since I last had the pleasure of seeing You I have begun to Ride & to Walk With great Success – in short to live a great deal out in the Air Without fatigue. all wh. has posibly been of use already & I feel Much stronger & better –

By persuing this plan With a Regular diet I am Very Sanguine in my hopes that My Health Will Shortly quite Recover & that I shall be in a better State of health than I have been in A great while – The Prince keeps me in Very good order & adheres As nearly to Your plan for me As possible –

As I had nothing particular to Say further than what I have here communicated to You I Would not plague You to come down to see me – whatever occurs You Shall instantly know –

Believe me to be
Your Sincere freind
Charlotte

This is the letter reproduced in Plate II, *a*, *b*, and *c*.

II

Sir Richard Croft's appointment

Letter of appointment as Surgeon in Ordinary to Princess Charlotte and Prince Leopold

Property of R. Page Croft Esq.,
of The Round House, Ware, Herts.

These are to certify, that Sir Richard Croft, Bart: is appointed Surgeon in Ordinary to Their Royal and Serene Highnesses, The Princess Charlotte, and The Prince Leopold; to have, hold and enjoy the said office – together with all rights privileges and advantages, thereunto belonging –

Claremont
November the third – one thousand
Eight hundred and Seventeen –
Robert Gardiner [13]
By Their R & S. H.H. Commands
[with their seal]

III

Pregnancy, labour and death

Seven documents

Property of R. Page Croft Esq.,
of The Round House, Ware, Herts.

I

Report of a consultation between Sir Richard Croft and Dr. Matthew Baillie on the 'plan or general Rules' for the Princess's management during her pregnancy (in Sir Richard's handwriting).

On talking over the particulars of Princess Charlotte's situation with Dr Baillie, we determined on the following plan or general Rules for her future management.

To rise at nine o'clock every morning & to breakfast by ten, but neither to eat Eggs or other Animal-food.

To take Luncheon about two o'clock, of Fruit, or sweetmeat, with Bread or Biscuit.

To take plain dressed Meat at dinner, & that which is the most easy of digestion, & not to exceed two glasses of Wine at and after dinner, & this to be the only Wine taken in the course of the day.

To take riding & walking exercise every day that the weather will permit, but not to such a degree as to cause fatigue.

To use the Shower bath every other day between breakfast & two o'clock, beginning with the Water a little tepid, & to have the Loins sponged with cold Water every morning.

2

The 'General rules' (in Dr. Baillie's handwriting).

For Princess Charlotte

To rise at Nine every morning

To take Breakfast before Ten

To eat a little cold meat, or some Fruit & Bread at Luncheon about Two

---

To take food plainly dress'd and easy of digestion at Dinner

Not to exceed two glasses of Wine at and after dinner –

To take exercise both by walking and on horseback, every day that the weather is favourable, but the exercise should not be violent –

To use the Shower bath every other day and to begin with water a little tepid –

To have the Loins spunged with cold water every day –

Endorsed: 'General rules for P–C–'

3

The history of the Princess's labour (in Sir Richard Croft's handwriting).

HRH. went into labour about seven o'clock on monday the third of Novr being forty two weeks & one day from her last recovery [10].

The Water began to come away between six & seven PM. & pains soon followed.

About eleven o'clock, I first made an examination, & found the Os Uteri open to the size of halfpenny, & the pains recuring about every 8 or 10 minutes.[1]

About three o'clock HRH. was seized with a violent retching, when, thinking it possible that might considerably expedite her labour, I thought it proper that the Council [14] should be informed that HRH. was in labour, & they all of

[1] Originally 'every ten minutes' and then 'every five minutes'.

them arrived by seven o'clock. Seeing that the pains were very insufficient, though the Os Uteri was at eleven o'clock on tuesday morning, dilated to the size of a crown piece & very thin, I suspected there might be Twins, or that from some other cause the Uterus was prevented from acting with vigour. Still the labour continued progressive, & at ab^t six in the evening the Os Uteri was all gone back, except just under the Pubis, & at nine o'clock it had perfectly retired, & for the first time I could feel an Ear of the Child.

As the pains still continued unusually feeble I thought it right to send off a letter written at eleven o'clock in the morning, to bring Dr Sims, it being before settled, that he was to be the consulting Man, in case such should be required. It had occured to me, that the pains might never become sufficiently strong, & powerful, & that assistance might ultimately become necessary, & I thought it would be improper to afford that assistance by the use of instruments, without a consultation.

Dr Sims arrived about two o'clock on Wednesday morning, when I proposed to mention it to HRH., but Baillie & Sims thought it unnecessary that Sims should see HRH., & therefore she was not told of his arrival.

From this time the labour continued progressive, but unusually slow, & the pains were less considerable than they are very generally at that period or stage of a labour.

At between three & four o'clock[1] on Wednesday evening, the Childs Head had began to press on the external parts, & it was born at nine o'clock by the action of HRH^s pains only. From about twelve o'clock on wednesday morning the Uterine discharge became of a dark green colour, which inclined us to suspect it possible the Child might be dead, & of course made us provide everything for its reanimation. When born it had no mark of life, the Navel String was very small & of a dark green or black colour. Brandy was put into the Childs Mouth & its lungs were inflated before the Navelstring was cut, & after every thing possible was attempted from the Aid of Warm-bath, inflation & rubing with Salt & Mustard, but no

[1] Originally 'At between six & seven o'clock'.

animation was ever restored, which made us suppose it had been dead some hours, or perhaps from the time of the green discharge.

I now very soon discovered that the Uterus was contracting irregularly, & that the afterbirth, or the greatest part of it, was retained[1] in its upper part. This suspision I told to Dr Sims about a quarter of an hour after the birth of the Child, & confirmed it at the end of half an hour, when both he & Dr Baillie agreed I must take it away.

This operation was done with much facility &[2] before much blood appeared to be lost, & for two hours afterwards or till about half past eleven o'clock I had no apprehension, as HRH took plenty of nourishment & made very few complaints, & had a pulse not exceeding a hundred.

A little before twelve o'clock HRH. became a little sick, & complained of singing noise in her Head, when I give her a little Camphor Mixture which she shortly after brought up, saying it was very apt to make her sick. After this HRH. took a cup of Tea & appeared to sleep[3] for about half an hour, when finding her becoming very irritable & restless, after speeking to D^r B & Dr S. I gave her twenty drops of Laudanum in Wine & Water. Before one o'clock D^r B & D S. saw HRH. & from that time till the scene closed at half past two we could only give Cordials & stimulants.

4

A corrected draft of the history of the Princess's labour (in unknown handwriting).

Her Royal Highness Princess Charlotte Augusta first began to show Symptoms of labour at seven o'Clock on the Evening of Monday the third of November, at the Expiration of forty two Weeks & two days, from H.R.H's earliest reckoning [10].

[1] Originally 'contained'.
[2] 'with much facility &' was added later.
[3] Originally 'attempted to sleep'.

During the first twenty hours, the pains were very sharp, acute, & distressing, returning at intervals of about eight minutes, and but little advancing the Labour.

The shape of H.R.H. was remarkably large for a first pregnancy, which circumstance, with the inefficacy of the pains, created a suspicion that there might be twins, or that the womb was acting with Some irregularity.

It had been arranged by H.R.H. some time previously to her Confinement, that in case a Consultation should be necessary, the Assistance of Dr Sims should be required.

The tardy progress of the Labour, giving reason to suppose, that unless the pains became more Efficacious in the Course of the next twelve or Eighteen hours, some assistance might be necessary, or some Circumstances might arise, which would render the Opinion of Dr Sims desirable, a letter was dispatched to him at nine o'Clock on Tuesday Evening requiring his immediate attendance.

At two o'Clock, A.M. on Wednesday, the period of the Arrival of Dr Sims at Claremont, H.R.H.'^s^ pains had become more Efficacious, and the Labour was advancing.

The particulars of H.R.H.'^s^ case were very accurately detailed to Dr Sims, and it was proposed by Sir R^d^ Croft that he should be immediately presented to H.R.H., but this proposal was objected to by Dr Baillie & Dr Sims, who considered the measure as unnecessary and unadviseable. Dr Sims remained in an adjoining room, where he regularly received information of the state and progress of the Labour, and was at hand to be admitted into the presence of H.R.H. whenever it might be thought necessary or advantageous. The Labour continued progressive, and at nine o'Clock at night, H.R.H. was, without any artificial assistance, delivered of a still born male child.

Instruments were in readiness[1] in case they might have been required, but the Employment of them never became a question, because the Labour, though proceeding slowly, advanced naturally.

H.R.H. took some repose in Bed during part of the nights of

[1] Originally: 'in the house' instead of 'in readiness'.

Monday, & Tuesday, was generally up, & frequently walking about the rooms during the day time, & remained up, untill a short time previous to her delivery. To this H.R.H. was encouraged by observing that the pains became less Efficacious when she was in a recumbent posture.

H.R.H. exhibited no marks of deficient strength during her Labour.

The greatest part of Wednesday, the Child was suspected to be dead, or if this were not the case, it appeared probable, that the Child might be found in a state of Suspended Animation at the time of its birth. Every known means for restoring animation had been prepared, were instantly used upon the birth of the Child, and continued without intermission, but they proved ineffectual.

Soon after the Birth of the Child, the suspicion which had been previously entertained of the irregular action of the Womb, was confirmed. The tardiness of the Labour was thus explained, & an unfavorable separation of the Afterbirth was expected. These circumstances were immediately communicated to Dr Sims.

At half past nine o'Clock, a discharge of blood took place. Dr Sims, who was then employed[1] in an adjoining room, in continuing the process of reanimating the Child, was instantly informed, & in consultation with Sir R^d^ Croft agreed that the immediate separation and removal of the afterbirth were necessary.

These were[2] accomplished with little difficulty[3] & followed by a very moderate[4] discharge of either fluid or coagulated blood. On the separation of the afterbirth the Womb con-

[1] Originally: 'At half past nine o'Clock, it was reported to Dr Sims that a discharge had begun, he was then employed'.

[2] Originally: 'The separation was'.

[3] Between 'difficulty' and 'followed' there was the following passage: 'and immediately after it was detached, H.R.H. had the strongest pain, witnessed during her labour, which forced the Afterbirth down where it was allowed to remain till near ten o'Clock, when as it caused inconvenience from being in part protruded, it was finally removed & was'.

[4] Originally 'little' instead of 'very moderate'.

tracted with more vigour & regularity than it had evinced during any part of the labour.[1]

The whole process of the labour was thus accomplished, & all circumstances appeared to be proceeding favourably. S^r^ R C. who had waited upon H R H. with^t^ ever retiring to rest, from the commencement of the labour to its final termination, still continued his attendance.[2]

H.R.H. continued[3] as well as Ladies usually are, after equally protracted Labours, she talked cheerfully and took frequently of mild nourishment.[4]

At a quarter before twelve, H.R.H. complained of being a little sick, and of a singing noise in her head.[5] In about a quarter of an hour HRH vomited. Mild nourishment was given,[6] the Stomach became composed, after which HRH. was tranquil, her pulse firm & steady, & less than a hundred in a minute.

Between half past twelve & a quarter before one, H.R.H. was suddenly attacked with spasmodic affection of the Chest,[7] extreme restlessness & great difficulty of breathing, attended with a very rapid, feeble, & irregular pulse. – The most active sup-

[1] The last sentence (in Sir Richard Croft's handwriting) was written in substitution of the phrase 'and at this time the womb felt to be moderately contracted.'

[2] This paragraph is in Sir Richard's handwriting.

[3] The words 'H.R.H. continued' were preceded by 'For an hour & half after this' [the separation of the afterbirth].

[4] The next paragraph read: 'During the whole of the Labour, Sir R^d^ Croft was very seldom out of H.R.H.'^s^ room, or one of the two adjoining rooms, for a quarter of an hour at a time; – from the time the Child was born, he was never absent from these three Rooms for five minutes at a time; – & from a quarter before twelve to the fatal termination, he was scarcely ever from her Bed-side.'

[5] Originally 'in her head' was followed by: 'after which she brought up some Camphor Mixture lately taken, took some nourishment, and had a firm, steady pulse, from ninety four to a hundred. From this time H.R.H. frequently dozed for five minutes at a time, appeared very composed, & took nourishment when she awoke.'

[6] Between 'was' and 'given' there was originally 'frequently' and then 'afterwards'.

[7] The addition 'spasmodic affection of the Chest' is in Sir Richard's handwriting.

port by Cordials, Nourishment, Antispasmodic & Opiate Medicines were administered at short intervals, under the Eye & direction of Dr Baillie, Dr Sims & Sir Richard Croft, but without Effect, and at half past two o'Clock, H.R.H. expired, five hours & a half after the birth of the Child.[1]

5

A more detailed history of the third stage of the Princess's labour (in unknown handwriting, dated and signed by Sir Richard Croft).

In about ten minutes after the birth of the Child, I informed Dr Sims, that I suspected the hour-glass contraction of the uterus, for that I could not feel the placenta, & the uterus continued high. We were agreed, that nothing ought to be done, unless a discharge came on, & at half an hour after the birth, a discharge did come on, & Dr Sims then agreed with me, that it was adviseable to remove the placenta.

[1] A further paragraph, in much smaller writing, was added after the post-mortem, which was done on Friday, 7 November (III, 6). It runs: 'The cause of H.R.H.'^{s} Death, as it was quite unexpected until half past twelve, so it is still somewhat obscure. The symptoms were such as precede Death from Haemorrhage, but the quantity of Blood lost was scarcely sufficient to create any alarm, being less than usual on such occasions, yet added to about a pound of Blood found in the Cavity of the Uterus, might have been enough to produce the unfavorable symptoms in so very excitable a Constitution. – It is most probable, that the two Ounces of Fluid, found in the pericardium, were poured out during the violence of the spasmodic Affection of the Chest, & if so, it must have had very great influence in preventing the Heart from recovering its regular & vigorous action, *& it is possible, it might have been deposited earlier, & thus have produced all the distressing symptoms, & have had more to do with the fatal issue, than has been imagined.*'

This whole paragraph was afterwards deleted, as were the phrases in Dr. Baillie's handwriting written in substitution for those underlined (here in italics): 'It is even possible that some part of it may have been deposited earlier, and may have contributed in a considerable degree to produce the symptoms which so rapidly proved fatal – '

The paragraph, in its original version, is reproduced verbatim (with the substitution of 'It is most possible' for 'It is most probable' in the 9th line) in Sir Eardley Holland's paper (p. 915) [8] as Sir Richard's comment on the case.

In passing my hand, I met with some blood in the uterus, but no difficulty till I got to the contracted part, & tho' it was contracted so as only to admit the points of three fingers, & had a portion of the placenta embraced by it, it readily gave way, so as to allow my hand to pass with tolerable Ease, & I afterwards peeled off near two thirds of the adhering placenta with considerable facility.

Immediately on its being separated, HRH complained of acute & Violent pain, & the upper part of the uterus contracting on my hand, I grasped the placenta, & gradually brought it down into the Vagina. – Leaving it there, I went again to D[r] Sims, & the Council [14], & reported what I had done.

On returning to H.R.H. I found her complaining of pain which recurred at intervals, & when these had continued to ten o'Clock, or from about twenty five minutes from the time the Placenta was left in the Vagina, as H.R.H. complained of it giving her great inconvenience, finding it considerably protruded, I ventured to take it away, and it was followed by very little, of either fluid blood, or coagulum.

At this time, as well as I could determine by feeling the abdomen through the Bandage, the uterus appeared moderately contracted.

Richard Croft
[Sunday] 9 Nov[r] 1817.

Endorsed: 'Afterbirth'

6

A copy of the post-mortem report (in unknown handwriting).

Copy.

The appearances which were observed on inspecting the Body of Her late Royal Highness The Princess Charlotte of Wales the seventh of November 1817.

The Membranes of the Brain had their natural appearance. The Vessells of the Pia Mater were less distended with Blood than was to be expected after so severe a Labour. The Ventricles of the Brain contained very little fluid. The Plexus Choroides was of a pale Colour, and the substance of the Brain had its natural texture.

The Pericardium contained two ou[ces] of red coloured fluid: The Heart itself and the Lungs were in a natural state. The Stomach contained nearly three Pints of liquid [15]. The Colon was distended with Air.

The small Intestines Spleen Pancreas & Kidneys were in a healthy state. The Uterus contained a considerable quantity of coagulated Blood and extended as high as the Navel, & the Hour Glass Contraction was still very apparent. The right Ovarium was formed into a Cyst the size of a Hen's Egg, distended with Serum, and a Mass of Sebaceous Matter, the left Ovarium was in a Healthy state.

The Urinary Bladder was empty & in a sound condition.

The Child was well formed and weighed nine pounds – Every part of its internal Structure was quite sound.

(Signed) David Dundas [16]
Everard Home [17]

Endorsed: 'Examination'

7

A copy of Dr. John Sims's postscript to the statement written by the three Doctors for the Members of the Royal Family (*in Sir Richard Croft's handwriting*).

As some of the above circumstances could not come under my immediate observation, not having seen her Royal Highness till symptoms of danger occured, I beg leave to add, that on my arrival at Claremont, Sir R[d] Croft proposed to mention it to HRH & to introduce me. The state of the labour at that time, precluded all thoughts of having recourse to any artificial assistance, therefore D[r] Baillie & I thought such introduction was then, both unnecessary & unadviseable.

As the labour continued from that time, to the end, progressive, there was no period of it, at which a question about the use of instruments could have been entertained. I was in the adjoining Room, the greatest part of the day, and was continually informed of the state & progress of the labour, & could have seen HRH. whenever it had been thought necessary.

When it was found that the afterbirth did not come away favourably, I was perfectly satisfied with S[r] R Crofts representation & quite agreed with him in the propriety of removing it. I was at that time still engaged in fruitless efforts to reanimate the Child; and the introduction of a stranger, at that moment, to the Royal Patient, as it appears to me, was particularly objectionable

John Sims

[Tuesday] 11th Nov[r] 1817

Copy. –

Endorsed: 'Sims's Report, in addition to the one [*v.* Note 32] signed by D[r] Baillie & Sir Rich[d] Croft.'

IV

Twelve letters, 8–28 November 1817

Ten letters to Sir Richard Croft,
the copy of one reply by him
and one letter to Lady Croft

Property of R. Page Croft Esq.,
of The Round House, Ware, Herts.

1

Sir Benjamin Bloomfield [18], *on behalf of the Prince Regent.*

Sir B: Bloomfield is honored with the Commands of the Prince Regent to convey to Sir Richard Crofts His Royal Highness's Acknowledgement of the zealous care and indefatigable attention manifested by Sir Richard towards His beloved Daughter during Her late eventful Confinement; And to express His Royal Highness's entire confidence in the medical skill & ability which he displayed, during the arduous and protracted Labour; whereof the issue, under the will of divine Providence, has overwhelmed His Royal Highness with such deep affliction.
Carlton House [Saturday] 8th November 1817

2

Sir David Dundas [16].

Richmond [Saturday] 8. Novr 1817.

Dear Sir.

you are so peculiarly connected with the late melancholy event, & your feelings so deeply wounded, that I am sure any circumstance which demonstrates the right sentiments of those most intimately concerned in it towards you, must be somewhat gratifying to you.

When Sir E: Home [17] & myself waited on the Prince Regent last night,[1] I was much pleased to hear him say, (when your distress was mentioned) that He was sure every thing which human Skill could do, had been done by you, that nothing could exceed the interest which you had shewn & that He considered the event as one of those dispensations of providence which could not be averted –

It is not my dear Sir that your reputation requires any protection, but I thought it might be agreable to you to know that it was properly considered in the highest quarter.

This communication I make to you in confidence, as you must be aware that what passes in such interviews ought not generally to be detailed – But having witnessed yesterday your deep affliction, I could not deny myself the satisfaction, which the circumstance mentioned presented, of endeavouring to diminish it.

I remain Dear Sir.

Yours faithfully.

David Dundas.

Addressed: 'Sir R[d] Croft. Bar[t]'

3

Lady Morpeth [19].

My dear Sir Richard

I am quite miserable at the sad sad intelligence this morning's post has brought and cannot express how much I feel for you –

I write partly to express my deep my heartfelt condolence & also to desire you not to think of answering my last letter which was totally without importance, & believe me ever most truly

Your obliged Friend

Georg[a] Morpeth

Castle Howard Saturday [8 November]

[1] After they had performed the post-mortem (Friday, 7 November; *v.* III, 6).

4

Colonel James Bathurst [20].

Somerleaze near Wells Somersetshire
[Saturday] 8th Novr 1817

My Dear Sir,

I trust you will acquit me of mere idle Curiosity in troubling you at this time with a few lines to enquire after you, but I am too much indebted to your Skill and kindness as well as attention to Lady Caroline and our children not to feel a more than common concern in every thing relating to you & as I have seen the Interest you take in those who are under your Charge, & therefore am aware how much you must have suffered on the late melancholy loss, at which all England I believe will deeply grieve, & which the knowledge of those more immediately round the Princess has made me perhaps still more bitterly lament, I cannot help wishing to hear that you have not materially suffered from the Anxiety, fatigue & feelings which must have a good deal affected you & If you could favor me with a line or that any of your family would act as your Secretary, either to Lady Caroline or myself I should be greatly obliged & should wish at the same time to learn how poor Mrs Campbell [21] has borne the loss of one who she had known & had the Charge of for so many years. If you should see her again pray remember me to her very kindly.

I will not intrude longer than to offer the very sincere good wishes of Lady Caroline & myself for the Welfare of yourself & all your family, & she will be most happy if our finances will allow of such a Journey if she should be so fortunate as again to have the benefit of your Care in the Spring for her third Confinement. She & her two Children are all quite well.

Believe me Dear Sir
yours very sincerely & obliged
James Bathurst

Addressed: 'Richard Croft Bart. Old Burlington St London'

5

Dr. Matthew Baillie.

Dear Croft,

I hope that you are less distress'd than when I last saw You, and that you are beginning to see the Circumstances in their real point of view –

I had a long conversation with the Queen last night and She was most perfectly satisfied with your Conduct and with that of the other medical men – All the other Branches of the Royal Family with whom I have conversed, and all the Members of the Houshold here have exactly the same opinion – They firmly believe that it was impossible for any Person to shew more judgement, or attention or Zeal than you did upon this most afflicting occasion –

I am firmly convinced that this is the opinion of the Public at large – It is quite obvious to a common Understanding that the attack was so sudden and violent as to be uncontroulable by all human Means – It had the violence of a hurricane –

I thought it proper to leave a Copy of the general Statement with the Queen, and I enclose another which you should carry to Carlton House for the Prince Regent. He will be displeas'd if any Member of the Royal Family should get a Statement, and Himself be omitted – This statement should be signed by You and D[r] Sims [*v.* Note 32] –

I am always Dear Croft
Yours very truly
M Baillie

Windsor Castle [Sunday] Nov[r] 9 – 1817

Addressed: 'Sir Rich[d] Croft'; endorsed: 'Baillie's Note'

6

Sir William Knighton [22].

Confidential

My Dear Sir Richard

You may rely on seeing me to Night about eight. When I

first saw the Prince to day, the Duchess of Gloucester [23] was present. Her R.H. is quite satisfied, and entered most minutely into the propriety of Your management during the whole period of P.C.'s pregnancy. In short nothing could be more satisfactory to Your feelings. *Immediately* after this, the P. Regent went down to Windsor to see the Queen. You have nothing to do, but to be quiet, and the whole thing will be satisfactorily got under.

I have seen three or four of the late Princess's great friends to day – The Marchioness of Worcester [24], Lady Anne Smith [24], &c – and I have satisfied them quite. – L^y^ Worcester promised me that she would write Lady Jersey [25] and say she had seen me.

Your sincere and very affectionate friend
W Knighton
Sunday 5½ [9 November]

7

Sir Robert Gardiner [13] *to Lady Croft.*

Claremont. [Sunday] Novr 9. 1817

My dear Madam

The distress of this house puts many duties out of our heads or I should sooner have written to you for accounts of Sir R Croft – I am unwilling to interrupt the quiet that I am happy to think he is restored to, by any questions at this moment – but I will trust to your kindness for giving me an account of him –

The Prince had a very calm night and is rather better this morning –

With my most kind regards and united good wishes of all here to Sir R Croft
Believe me My dear Madam
Your most faithful
Robert Gardiner

Endorsed: 'Gardiner'

8

Sir Benjamin Bloomfield [18], *on behalf of the Prince Regent.*

Sir Benjamin Bloomfield presents his Compliments to Sir Richard Crofts and requests that he will have the goodness to be at Carlton House this day at two o'Clock[1]
Carlton House [Wednesday] 12 Novr 1817.

Endorsed: 'Bloomfield.'

9

Dr. Christian Stockmar [26].

My dear Sir.

I have thankfully received yesterday evening Your letters, the report and the book, You have been kind enough to send to me.

It is no small satisfaction to me, that I had full opportunity of forming an opinion of Your professional and private caracter long before this last and dreadful event happened. From the first moment after H.R.H. death till now I was and I am completely convinced, that nothing was omitted, that ought to have been done.

Not forgetting however my age[2] and that my knowledge of midwifery is only a theoretical one, I am fully aware how very little comfort my professional opinion may afford You. Perhaps You might lay a greater weight upon the assurance that I feel the sincerest friendship for You, that I value truth more than life and that I shall hold it my particular duty to maintain her standard in this present case, even against its slightest deviation.

The poor Prince eats almost nothing and scarcely sleeps, his health however is not materially altered, and he does in fact as it might have been expected. He speaks with the highest esteem of You and Your attachment shown to him and partakes sincerely of Your disappointment and present distress.

[1] Nothing else is known about this summons.

[2] He was 30 years old, Sir Richard Croft 55.

I inclose in the mean time as I promissed a copy of the statement [*v*. Note 32] You did leave in my hands.

God bless You, I hope You and Your family are perfectly well and beg You will believe me My dear Sir

most sincerely and faithfully Yours

D. Chr. Stockmar.

Claremont [Friday] 14th Nov. 1817.

10

Sir Richard Croft to Dr. Stockmar [26] (*copy, in unknown handwriting*).

Sunday 16 November 1817 Old Burlington Street

My dear Sir,

It is to me the greatest consolation, to find that I have in the hearts and understanding of those in whom I have placed my confidence, a cordial return, and your letter received last night, is in this respect, a great consolation to my feelings.

You have been for some time intimately acquainted with the amiable disposition of the illustrious individual, whom we, in common with the whole nation, deplore; to me, an intimate knowledge of her excellence, is recent, but the impression must ever remain permanent.

The very kind and candid expression, of your opinion upon this case, is in the highest degree consolatory; and the noble assurance, that you will maintain the standard of truth, in the present case against the slightest deviation, is an instance, of disinterested friendship, offered where it is likely to be most useful.

You and I who have witnessed the amiable virtues of our good Prince, & those of the exalted and amiable individual, whom he has lost cannot be surprised at the continuance of his affliction. I hope He does not consider me, as negligent, or inattentive, in not having personally made my enquiries at Claremont, but in truth, I have been ill able to encounter the exertion, necessary for the business, I have been called upon, to do; much less have I been able to support the painful feelings, which a view of Claremont would revive. In a very few days however, I hope & trust to be able to pay my personal respects. Should you ever bring my name before our good Prince, let me beg of you to present my respectful duty and sincere thanks, for his kind recollection and solicitude about me, and remember me most respectfully to the rest of your afflicted party.

In the sincere hope that you may some day afford me the pleasure of introducing you to my family, and of consolidating the friendship that exists between us, believe me, my dear Sir,

Yours most sincerely, and faithfully,

Endorsed: 'To Dr Stockmar'

II

Sir Robert Gardiner[13], *on behalf of Prince Leopold.*

Claremont [Sunday] November the 23^d 1817

My dear Sir

The Prince Leopold was unable previous to His return from Windsor,[1] to attempt any offer of H S H thanks to you, for all your care, your indefatigable zeal and attention, during your late arduous attendance at Claremont –: H S H avails himself of the earliest possible moment, to convey to you His assurance that throughout those dreadful circumstances we deplore, He must always remember with what earnest endeavors you fulfilled your professional duties – and, in the general sorrow, which circumstances have rendered peculiarly an affliction to you, to assure you of His unalterable sense and confidence, in all your efforts to avert it.

Believe me with unfeigned regard My dear Sir
Your most faithful and obedient Servant
Robert Gardiner

Addressed: 'To Sir Richard Croft. Bart: Old Burlington Street'

[1] For the funeral (Tuesday, 18 November, and Wednesday, 19 November).

Sir Benjamin Bloomfield [18], *on behalf of the Prince Regent.*

Sir B: Bloomfield presents his Compliments to Sir Richard Crofts and has the honor to return to him the inclosed Letter conveying the sentiments entertained by Prince Leopold of Sir Richards professional skill and exertions, (as exemplified during his attendance on the late Princess Charlotte). And Sir B: Bloomfield having had the honor to lay the Letter before the Prince Regent has to acquaint Sir Richard that His Royal Highness expressed great satisfaction in the accordance of Prince Leopolds sentiments with His own.
Carlton House [Friday] 28th Nov: 1817

V

Princess Charlotte to Dr. Matthew Baillie

The Royal College of Surgeons of England,
Hunter Baillie Collection [27], vol. III, p. 69, document 49

Dear Dr Bailly –

It is the Princes wish as well as mine, that You should *Yourself*, Either *alone*, or together with Sr Richard Crofts (should *You prefer* it, & think it better) go, both to the Queen & the Prince Regent, & inform them of the cause that will Necessarily make my attendance at the Drawing Room *impossible*. *You* must be the *best judge*, if the matter can be *officially announced* in the present state of affairs to them or whether the *simple facts* as they are, *should only be told*, & the *conjectures left to them to make* –

The Prince will of course be in Town on Wednesday to attend the Drawing Room, but I shall *not come up at all*, As I was fatigued after my last journey –

I have to thank You for having called upon me, & to offer You my regrets at not having had the pleasure of seeing You –

Believe me to be My Dear Dr Bailly
Ever Your Most sincere friend
Charlotte

[Monday] April 21st Clermont 1817[1]

[1] Three months and nine days, or 14 weeks and one day, 'from her last recovery' (12 January), according to III, 3 [10].

VI

Count Münster to the Duke of Cambridge

Count Münster [28], *Hanoverian Minister in London, to the Duke of Cambridge, at that time Viceroy of Hanover*

Niedersächsisches Staatsarchiv, Hannover, Dep. 84, Hann. 9
Domestica Nr. 200

London, [Friday] November 7th, 1817.
N. 514 pr – 13 – ——N 75 cod.

Most gracious Duke, highly esteemed Colleagues,

Your Royal Highness and my highly esteemed Colleagues will share the grief of our Most Gracious Regent, the whole Royal Family and the Country on the loss of Her Royal Highness the Princess Charlotte, by her marriage Duchess of Saxe-Coburg.

Her decease, as grievous as it was unexpected, occurred on the 6th of this month at 2 a.m., several hours after a difficult labour and the birth of a still-born male child.

Before this bereavement the Prince Regent had been for some 10 days at a country seat in the County of Suffolk [29], 96 English miles from London, whither I had accompanied His Royal Highness.

The first official notice of the onset of the labour, when it had already lasted 27 hours, was received by His Royal Highness at about 0.30 p.m. on the 5th. He immediately drove back to London. A second messenger missed His Royal Highness during the night on the road. He arrived at Carlton House after 3 a.m., one hour after the demise of the Princess, which meanwhile became known before His Royal Highness could prepare himself for his journey to Clermont.

The death of the Princess was so unexpected that the

Ministers present [14] had left, and also the Prince of Coburg, her husband, had gone to bed on the advice of the doctors.

The sad news of the death of the Princess was conveyed to me in an official letter from Earl Bathurst, and the enclosed special edition of the Court Gazette[1] was immediately published.

This death, as Your Royal Highness and my esteemed Colleagues will themselves realize, has very important political consequences. The British Crown will not pass to the House of Saxe, as previously seemed probable, and Hanover has the prospect of being longer subject, with this realm, to the same master [30].

It will be a comfort to Your Royal Highness and my esteemed Colleagues to learn that our Gracious Prince Regent is in as good health as is possible in these circumstances.

I remain with the greatest reverence and the most perfect regard,

Your Royal Highness's and my highly esteemed Colleagues' respectful and most obedient servant.

E.v. Münster

Addressed: 'To the Royal Ministry Hanover'

The German original is written in a neat clerical hand in Gothic lettering, except the English proper names. The last line and the signature are in Count Münster's handwriting.

[1] *The London Gazette Extraordinary*, Number 17302 (2265) of Thursday, November 6th, 1817.

VII

Mrs. Baillie's notebook [31]

The Royal College of Surgeons of England,
Hunter Baillie Collection [27], vol. VIII, p. 41, leaves 13–20

The few remaining letters to be here given are relating to the Royal Family, and some of them at least may perhaps be found interesting from their connection with an event which spread such deep and sincere affliction over the whole English Nation.

I

To Mrs Baillie [From Dr. Baillie]

My dearest Sophy

Princess Charlotte bore a dead Child at nine o'clock last night, was quite well till a little after twelve, and died at half past two this morning. – Difficulty of breathing, spasms, extreme restlessness came on, and she very soon died. – I imagine that her case very much resembled that of Mrs Cavendish. –

I came to town to have a conversation with the Prince Regent, who is quite satisfied that no medical error was committed. – I am now in Burlington Street,[1] return to Claremont immediately, and shall be at Wentworths[2] I hope to-morrow afternoon in my way to Windsor.

Prince Leopold is bearing his misfortune like a Man, but is evidently very deeply affected. – Sir Richard Croft is very low, but I hope will soon be better. I have hardly had any sleep since I have seen you, but except for fatigue, and such melancholy

[1] Sir Richard Croft's home.

[2] Wentworths, Virginia Water, was a country residence occupied in the summer and autumn by Dr. Baillie and his family.

feelings as such an event must inspire, I am as well as usual – My love to every body –

I am always, my dearest Girl,
Yours most affectionately
M Baillie –

Old Burlington Street Thursday Novr 6 – 1817 –

Your Sister[1] is pretty well.

2

Some particulars of the case of H.R.H. Princess Charlotte, written for the satisfaction of the Royal Family [32].

The labour of Her Royal Highness, Princess Charlotte, began at seven o'clock on Monday evening of the third of November, 1817, and terminated at nine o'clock on Wednesday [evening][2], the fifth of November, in the birth of a still-born Male Child. – The labour therefore continued during fifty hours. [The exertions of the Uterus were feeble throughout the greater part of the labour, but during the last few hours they were stronger, and more satisfactory.]

As the labour was very tedious, Dr Sims was sent for by Sir Richard Croft, on Tuesday evening, and arrived at Claremont about two o'clock on Wednesday morning. He concurred entirely in opinion with Sir Richard Croft respecting the situation of Her Royal Highness, and that as long as the labour was making progress, [al]though slowly, the conduct of it should be left to nature. – Instruments were at hand [to assist the Uterus], if it were thought adviseable to employ them.

During the whole of this very tedious labour Her Royal Highness was cheerful, looked well, and Her pulse was good.

[1] Lady Croft, her twin.

[2] The words and phrases in square brackets are taken from another copy of this statement, also in Mrs. Baillie's handwriting, in the Hunter Baillie Collection [27] at the Royal College of Surgeons of England (vol. VIII, p. 45). Possibly it was written in 1817 and the text of the notebook was copied from it.

Her Royal Highness often walked about the rooms, and was very little on Her bed.

The Child was born, as before mentioned, at nine o'clock in the evening, and as [upon examination, an hour-glass contraction of the Uterus was discovered, Sir Richard Croft, with the concurrence of D[r] Sims, took away the after-birth at twenty minutes before ten.] –

Her Royal Highness appeared quite as well as Women commonly do after so tedious a labour, and much better than they often do under such circumstances, till about a quarter before twelve at night. Her Royal Highness then complained of some sickness, and singing in her ears. Soon after H.R.H. threw up a little fluid, which seemed chiefly the Camphor mixture she had swallowed. She then became a little irritable, and began to talk too much.

About a quarter before one She complained of great uneasiness in her chest, and She began to breathe with great difficulty. Her pulse was very feeble and irregular, and She became extremely restless, not being able to remain a single moment in the same posture. This very alarming state continued, and kept encreasing, till half past two in the morning, when Her Royal Highness expired. – Her mind was entire throughout the whole of this dreadful attack, but there was no reason to suppose that H.R.H. was aware of her own danger.

The Child had been born dead, but it appeared not to have been dead long. The most strenuous efforts were made to reanimate it by means that had been previously provided, but they were unavailing. Some circumstances had rendered it probable that the Child would be still-born, and therefore every means of recovery were in readiness.

The Child was perfectly formed, and weighed nine pounds.

M Baillie

November – 1817 –

The following memorandum has been found in his own writing – 'In looking back very often upon this most distressing event I am convinced that Sir Richard Croft did all that the melancholy case admitted of, and that the Princess Charlotte's life would not have been saved by any different treatment.' [33]

3

To Sir Richard Croft, Bar^{t}. [From Sir Benjamin Bloomfield [18], *on behalf of the Prince Regent*]

[Omitted; it is a copy of IV, 1]

4

To Dr Baillie. From the domestic Physician of H.R.H.[1] *Prince Leopold.* [*Dr. C. Stockmar*] [26]

Dear Sir

I received your note of 20th Novr this morning. Thank God, Prince Leopold does as well as we can possibly expect him to be with such sorrow and fatigue, as he has gone through. He took an airing on horseback yesterday, and the day before.

He certainly cherishes his grief by every mean which remembrance of former days may afford, but there is no want, nor use I think, to interfere about it with a soul so noble and strong as the Prince's.

The Prince commands me to remember Him with great affection to You.

With the best wishes for your health, I remain Dear Sir,

Your sincerely faithful Servant

C. Stockmar.

Saturday *Novr 22.* 1817.

5

To Sir Richard Croft. [*From Sir Robert Gardiner* [13], *on behalf of Prince Leopold*]

[Omitted; it is a copy of IV, 11]

[1] H.S.H. (His Serene Highness) would have been correct.

6

To Dr Baillie. [*From Dr. C. Stockmar*] [26]

Dear Sir

I received your note of 27th Novr yesterday. I can't say there is any amendment in the Prince's state of mind. He is not ill, but I must confess the strong apprehensions to you I have sometimes, He might become so.

He does not eat much, yet quite enough to support the frame, but there is an increased irritability about him which prevents him from sleeping, and he commonly remains awake the greater part of the night. He don't like to stir, and it always costs some trouble to get him a little out of the house.

You know that he is about to go for some time to Weymouth. Perhaps the change of air and scene will do him good.

The Prince's kind regards to you. – I wish you may do well yourselves, and believe that I am, with true love and esteem, my dear Sir,

Your obedient Servant

C. Stockmar.

Claremont. [Monday] 1st Decr 1817.

7

To Dr Baillie. [*From Dr. C. Stockmar*] [26]

Dear Sir

Having received your note of 2d inst. I did not fail to give your dutiful respects to Prince Leopold, and to acquaint Him what the Princess of Wales had charged you with [*v.* No. 8, § 2]. H.R.H.[1] is much obliged to you, and commands me to offer you His kindest regards.

There was some few weeks past, a moment when the Prince began to feel a little better, when he got violent rheumatick pains in the face, which, by the total want of appetite, the acuteness of the pains, and the restlessness, reduced Him more than he was ever before. He is certainly very emaciated, and is

[1] H.S.H.

still far from paying any attention to any thing but to the remembrance of his lost friend. Did I not trust on His being so very young, and on the great command He has over Himself, no doubt I should be alarmed sometimes.

Our going to Weymouth, which is to take place to-morrow, may I hope contribute to his improvement. I shall feel pleasure in giving you an account of the Prince's health some time hence from Weymouth. – With the warmest wishes for your welfare, I remain, Dear Sir,

Your very faithful Servant

C. Stockmar. –

Claremont [Sunday] 4th Jan. 1818.

8

To Dr Baillie. From H.R.H. the Princess of Wales.

What an awful event commands me to write to you, my only true friend I have left in England! – England, that proud country, has lost every thing in losing my ever beloved Daughter, and I have not only to lament a darling of a Child, but my only truly warm and attached friend – I have not lost her, she is only gone before, and I trust that soon I shall meet her again in a much better world than the present one.

Pray, for heaven's sake, send me a most exact account of all what concerns this dreadful event, and I am much afraid some mistake must have occurred, that such melancholy event could take place. Give also my most affectionate love and respect to the dear Prince Leopold, and I trust we shall once meet that I may have the comfort to know every detail of her happiness and comfort, which she, the beloved departed spirit enjoyed for some time with him. I can say no more, my heart is so full, and my poor head so weak. –

Believe me for ever, Your sincere friend,

C.P. –

Villa Capsielle.[1] Pesaro. [Tuesday] the 2nd of December – 1817 –

[1] Villa Caprile, near Pesaro, a town on the Adriatic, between Rimini and Ancona. The Princess of Wales had been living there since August 1817.

9

To Her Royal Highness, the Princess of Wales. [*From Dr. Baillie*]

Madam

I sympathize most deeply with Your Royal Highness in your present overwhelming affliction – I have never witnessed so distressing a scene, which has not only deprived You of an only Child, but has spread universal sorrow over this Nation. – Princess Charlotte and Prince Leopold were beloved in their neighbourhood, and respected by the whole Nation, which looked forward to Prosperity and Happiness under their Rule. It is impossible to describe the deep-felt sorrow of Prince Leopold, or the respect in which He is held by the Country. – His grief may be mitigated by time, but it will never leave Him.

This very sad Event seems to have been an infliction of Providence, for it was quite unexpected, and has not arisen from any Error in the treatment of Her Case.

Princess Charlotte had enjoyed more than Her usual health previous to her labour. The labour was exceedingly tedious, for it lasted fifty hours, but it was attended with no unusual circumstances, except [a slight contraction of the womb, retarding the passing away of the after-birth][1] which had happened in Your Royal Highness's own case, at the birth of Princess Charlotte.

The Princess was well for more than three hours after the labour. She was then suddenly seized with uneasiness in Her Chest, great difficulty of breathing, extreme restlessness, and had a very rapid, feeble, and irregular pulse. Sir Richard Croft, Dr Sims, and myself endeavoured to support Her sinking frame

[1] The phrases in square brackets are from R. Hingston Fox's letter written to the Editor of *The Lancet* on 14 November 1917 ('Sir Richard Croft and the case of the Princess Charlotte', **2:** 804, No. 4917, Nov. 24, 1917). Fox wrote: 'Dr. Matthew Baillie's own account of the occurrence . . . is taken from a manuscript letter which has been preserved, addressed to the Princess's mother'. I do not know where he found the letter or its copy. So far I have not succeeded in locating either, nor the original of the Princess of Wales's letter.

with every kind of Cordial, but all our efforts were unavailing. The symptoms were too violent to be controuled by any human means, and the Princess died in two hours from the beginning of the attack. –

Sir Richard Croft was indefatigable in his attention and zeal throughout the whole of this very sad business. He never quitted for more than a few minutes at a time the bed-chamber of the Princess, from the beginning of her labour until She expired.

The Child was a Male, well-formed, and still-born. Every attempt was made to reanimate him as soon as he was born, but without success.

This is an exact account of all the circumstances. We shall ever have to deplore the great calamity itself, but it could not have been prevented. [About a pint of coagulated blood was found by examination in the womb] and two ounces of water were found in the bag surrounding the heart. These may in some measure account for the fatal event. The first may have produced considerable weakness, and the second would produce the great feebleness and irregularity of the heart's action, which may have prevented Her Royal Highness's recovery.

I remain, Madam, with sincere sympathy, and a sense of humble duty,

Your Royal Highness's very humble Servant

M Baillie.

[Wednesday] Decr 24th – 1817 –

This unfortunate Princess, afterwards for a short time Queen of England, returned to this country in June 1820, after an absence of six years, and died at Brandenburgh House, Hammersmith, on Tuesday, August 7th, 1821, after circumstances but too well known and too certainly remembered. – Dr Baillie, then at his house in [Duntisbourne Abbots] Gloucestershire, was summoned to attend Her, in consultation with Dr Ainslie [34], Dr Maton [35], Dr Warren [36], and Dr Holland

[37], and the following mention of her death is taken from his letters. – Her complaint was inflammation of the bowels, believed to have been occasioned by the unhappy efforts which She persisted in making to be present at the Coronation of His Majesty in opposition to the strongest advice & most urgent entreaties of Her legal advisers and the consequent agitation of Her mind, in weather most intensely hot.

10

To Mrs Baillie. [*From Dr. Baillie*]

'I arrived at Brandenburgh House to-day at half past Two o'clock, and have seen the Queen. Her Majesty is still in a very precarious state, but is a little better than She was yesterday' – Monday, August 6. – 1821 – half past three.

Other documents

It was originally my intention to publish these documents as an appendix to a book on Princess Charlotte which I began writing a few years ago.

Unfortunately the time I can spare for historical studies is so limited and the bibliographical material I have collected is so large that my book will not be finished for some years yet, and I did not want to leave the documents unpublished for so long.

In this preliminary paper I have avoided any comment and conclusion; its only purpose is to lay all the available evidence on Princess Charlotte's labour and death before anyone who may be interested in the subject.

Under the heading '*The Authentic Documents*' Sir Eardley Holland (pp. 908–909) [8] listed:

1. 'The reports published three weeks after the events in the two chief London medical journals.' In his List of Authorities (p. 919) [8] Sir Eardley only quoted *The London Medical Repository* ('Case of the late Princess Charlotte of Wales', **8:** 534–537, No. 48, December 1817). An abridged version appeared in *The Times* of December 2, and later the account was printed in a pamphlet (*v.* No. 33, p. 61).

'Her Royal Highness the Princess Charlotte' was published in *The London Medical and Physical Journal* (**38:** 513–516, No. 226, December 1817).

Two long articles appeared in *The Monthly Gazette of Health; or, Popular Medical, Dietetic, and General Philosophical Journal*: 'Case of the late Princess Charlotte of Wales' (**2:** 732–744, No. 24, Dec. 1, 1817) and 'Case of the late Princess of Wales' (**3:** 760–768, No. 25, Jan. 1, 1818).

The Editors of a fourth Journal wrote: 'In answer to our numerous Correspondents, who complain of our not noticing the case of the lamented Princess Charlotte of Wales, we must reply, that as no authentic statement of the facts has yet been given by those who are competent to do it, the medical gentlemen in attendance, we are unwilling to fill our pages with mere *newspaper gossip*' (*The Medico-Chirurgical Journal and Review*, **5:** 89, No. 25, January 1818).

2. 'The statement written at the time "for the satisfaction of the Royal Family."' (*v.* VII, 2, III, 7, Plate III and Note 32).

3. 'A long letter written by Sims on 15th November, 1817, to Dr. Joseph Clarke, of Dublin' [38]. It runs:

London, [Saturday] November 15, 1817.

My dear Sir,

I do not wonder at your wishing to have a correct statement of the labour of Her Royal Highness, Princess Charlotte, the fatal issue of which has involved the whole nation in distress. You must excuse my being very concise, as I have been, and am very much hurried. I take the opportunity of writing this in a lying-in chamber.

Her Royal Highness's labour commenced by the discharge of the liquor amnii about 7 o'clock on Monday evening, and pains followed soon after; they continued through the night and a great part of the next day, sharp, short, but very ineffectual. Towards the evening Sir Richard Croft began to suspect that the labour might not terminate without artificial assistance, and a message was dispatched for me.

I arrived at two on Wednesday morning. The labour was now advancing more favourably, and both Doctor Baillie and myself concurred in the opinion that it would not be advisable to inform Her Royal Highness of my arrival. From this time to the end of the labour, the progress was uniform, though very slow, the patient in good spirits, pulse calm, and there never was room to entertain a question about the use of instruments.

About six in the afternoon the discharges became of a green colour which led to a suspicion that the child might be dead; still the giving assistance was quite out of the question, as the pains now became more effectual, and the labour proceeded regularly though slowly.

The child was born, without artificial assistance, at 9 o'clock in the evening. Attempts were for a good while made to reanimate it by inflating the lungs, friction, hot bath, &c., but without effect; the heart could not be made to beat even once.

Soon after the delivery Sir Richard Croft discovered that the uterus was contracted in the middle, in the hour-glass form, and, as some hemorrhage commenced, it was agreed that the placenta should be brought away by introducing the hand. This was done about half an hour after the delivery of the child, with more ease and less loss of blood than usual.

Her Royal Highness continued well for about two hours; she then complained of being sick at stomach, and of noise in her ears; began to be talkative, and her pulse became frequent, but I understand she was very quiet after this, and her pulse calm.

About half-past 12 o'clock she complained of severe pain at her chest, became extremely restless, with a rapid, irregular, and weak pulse. At this time I saw her for the first time, and saw immediately that she must die. It has been said we were all gone to bed, but that is not a fact. Croft did not leave the room, Dr. Baillie retired about eleven, and I went to my bed-chamber and laid down in my clothes at twelve.

By dissection, some bloody fluid (two ounces) was found in the pericardium, supposed to be thrown out in articulo mortis. The brain and other organs all sound except the right ovarium which was distended into a cyst, the size of a hen's egg; the hour-glass contraction of the uterus still visible; a considerable quantity of blood in the cavity of the uterus, but those present differ about the quantity, so much as from 12 ounces to a pound and a half; the uterus extending as high as the navel.

The cause of Her Royal Highness's death is certainly somewhat obscure; the symptoms were such as attend death from hemorrhage, but the loss of blood did not appear to be sufficient to account for a fatal issue. It is possible that the effusion into the pericardium took place earlier than what was supposed, and it does not seem to me to be quite certain that this might not be the cause.

As far as I can judge, the labour could not have been better managed. That I did not see Her Royal Highness more early was awkward; and it would have been better that I should have been introduced before the labour was expected; and it should have been understood that when the labour came on I should be sent to without waiting to know whether a consultation was necessary or not. I thought so at the time, but I could not propose such an arrangement to Croft. But this is entirely *entre nous*.

I am glad to hear that your son is well, and, with all my family, wish to be remembered to him; we were happy to hear that he was agreeably married.

I remain, my dear Doctor,
Ever yours, most truly,
Jno. Sims.

P.S. This letter is confidential, as, perhaps, I might be blamed for writing any particulars without the permission of Prince Leopold.

'The New Croft Papers', as Sir Eardley Holland named those which had been recently discovered (*v.* p. 3), were listed by him (pp. 912–913) [8] 'under three headings':

(1) 'A number of letters written by Croft in 1790 from Paris, when he was an aspiring young accoucheur of 28, in attendance on Georginiana [sic], Duchess of Devonshire, for her third confinement – when "the bachelor Duke" was born.' These letters have nothing to do with Princess Charlotte and will be the subject of another paper.

(2) 'Nine letters written by Charlotte to Croft and Baillie during pregnancy.' The nine letters presumably written to Sir Richard, because they were found among his family's papers, are printed here under heading I, the letter written to Dr. Baillie under heading V. This last letter is in the Hunter Baillie Collection [27] at the R.C.S. and not among 'The New Croft Papers'.

(3) 'This group ... comprises four documents: (*a*) Croft's personal record of the labour [*v*. III, 3]... (*b*) His reflections on the general course of labour and his views on the cause of death [*v*. III, 4]. (*c*) His prenatal instructions on diet and exercise [*v*. III, 1 and 2]. (*d*) A copy of the post-mortem report [*v*. III, 6].'

The 'three bulletins' and the 'extra bulletin' mentioned by Sir Eardley Holland (p. 909) [8] appeared at random in the newspapers for Wednesday, Thursday and Friday, November 5th, 6th and 7th; all are extremely laconic. Those signed by the three Doctors are four (Wednesday 5th, 8 a.m., 5.30 p.m., 9.15 p.m. and 10 p.m.); the 'extra bulletin' 'of less authority', from the 'Court news man', is dated Wednesday 5th, 4 p.m.

The 'notice in the *London Gazette*' (Holland, p. 909) [8] is referred to in note [1] to document VI. The two 'semi-medical "letters from Claremont"' written by the 'Court news man' after the Princess's death (Thursday, November 6th, 6 a.m. and 9 a.m.) can be found in *The Sun* for Thursday 6th (the second one) and Friday 7th (the first one) and in *The Times* for Friday 7th (both).

Sir Eardley Holland (p. 919) [8] quoted two books and two pamphlets published in the first months after Princess Charlotte's death: Green, Huish, Foot's first letter and Foot's second letter. They are No. 22, 25, 20 and 21 in the following list of books and pamphlets printed in that period, of which I own either the original (OR) or the complete photocopy (PH). Some of these publications are very rare.

Books and pamphlets 1817–1818

1

ACKLAND [Acland], James – *A monody on the lamented death of the Princess Charlotte Augusta of Wales, and of Saxe Coburg-Saalfeld.* By James Ackland, author of 'True patriotism,' and other poems. (London: Printed for the author, by John Rowe, 16, 'Change Alley, Cornhill; and sold by E. Wilson, 88, Royal Exchange; and J. Blacklock, 92, Royal Exchange. 1817.)

OR; B.M. 11641. f. 69. (14.); circa 22 × 14 cm; 14 pp.

2

ANON [J. Coote] – *A biographical memoir of the public and private life of the much lamented Princess Charlotte Augusta of Wales and Saxe-Coburg: illustrated with recollections, anecdotes, and traits of character, including incidental observations upon persons and events connected with the subject of the memoir; accompanied by explanatory and authentic documents in an appendix.* (London: Printed by J. Barfield, Wardour-Street, Printer to H.R.H. the Prince Regent, for John Booth, Duke-Street, Portland-Place; Hatchard, Piccadilly; Egerton, Whitehall; Rodwell & Martin, Bond-St; Chapple, Pall-Mall; and Longman, Hurst, Rees, Orme and Brown, Paternoster-Row. 1817.)

OR; B.M. 610. i. 7. (1.); circa 22 × 14 cm; viii (preceded by title and one blank page) + 340 pp.; 3 plates. Pages 47 and 48 are lacking, but there is no gap in the text; between p. 46 and p. 49 are inserted pp. *33 and 34*, which should have been placed between p. 34 and p. 35.

(2a) Id., Second Edition, 1817. The list of the publishers also includes Booker. OR; B.M. 195. c. 8.; x (including title and one blank page) + 344 pp.; 4 plates.

3

ANON – Hone's Edition. The whole of the burial procession and obsequies. *A most correct account of the funeral of the Princess Charlotte, in St. George's Chapel, Windsor.* (London: Printed by and for William Hone, 67, Old Bailey, three doors from Ludgate Hill. 1817. Price Sixpence.)

OR; circa 22 × 14 cm; 16 pp.; 1 plate.

(3a) Id., Second Edition, 1817. PH. The B.M. Catalogue lists the 3rd Edition, 1817: 1200. d. 16. (4.) (The whole, etc.).

4

ANON – Hone's Edition. *Authentic memoirs of the life of the late lamented Princess Charlotte; with clear statements showing the succession to the crown, and the probability of the wife of Jerome Buonaparte becoming Queen, and her son, Jerome Napoleon, being Prince of Wales, and afterwards King of these realms.* (London: Printed by and for William Hone, 67, Old Bailey, three doors from Ludgate Hill. 1817. Price Sixpence.)

PH; B.M. 10805. cc. 7.; 16 pp.; 1 plate. The B.M. Catalogue also lists the 3rd and 4th Editions, 1817: 10805. cc. 18. (1.) and 1200. d. 16. (1.).

5

ANON – Hone's Edition. *Authentic particulars of the death of the Princess Charlotte and her infant.* (London: Printed by and for William Hone, 67, Old Bailey, three doors from Ludgate Hill. 1817. Price Sixpence.)

PH; B.M. 09525. l. 33. (18.); circa 22 × 14 cm; 16 pp.; 1 plate.

(5a) Id., Third Edition, 1817. OR; B.M. 10601. tt. 11. (1.).

(5b) Id., Fifth Edition, 1817. OR; B.M. 1200. d. 16. (3.).

6

ANON – *Ceremonial for the private interment of Her late Royal*

Highness the Princess Charlotte-Augusta daughter of His Royal Highness the Prince Regent and consort of His Serene Highness the Prince Leopold of Saxe-Cobourg in the Royal Chapel of St. George at Windsor on Wednesday evening the 19th of November 1817.

OR; B.M. 1879. c. 1. (2.); circa 31 × 21 cm; 7 unnumbered pages; Coe, Printer, Little Carter Lane, Doctors' Commons. [1817].

7

ANON – *Memoir of the illustrious and amiable Princess Charlotte of Wales and Saxe-Coburg, who died Nov. 6, 1817; containing numerous anecdotes of her early life; an account of her happy union with Prince Leopold; her residence at Claremont; her last illness, and sudden and lamented death; a description of the funeral ceremonies; and a collection of characters, selected from the most elegant and well-written eulogies that have appeared: with a variety of other particulars, highly interesting to every British subject.* In two volumes. Vol. I. 'Oh, early lost! just loved, and snatched away! Politely learned, and elegantly gay! Blest with each charm the British heart to gain, To all most dear – to England dear in vain!' (London: Printed by and for R. Edwards, Crane Court, Fleet Street; and sold by all booksellers. 1818.)

OR; circa 22 × 14 cm; 8 + ccxcviii pp.; 1 plate. Vol. II: 5 + 296 pp.

8

ANON – *Memoirs of Prince Leopold, from his first arrival in England; with a variety of anecdotes of the Princess Charlotte, now first collected.* By the Editor of Hone's Editions of the 'Life,' 'Death,' & 'Funeral,' of Her Royal Highness, to which this publication is a sequel. [Vignette: The Princess's burial place] 'After the ceremony of the interment, the Prince descended into the mausoleum alone, and wept over the remains of his departed consort upwards of an hour.' . . . Page 10. (London: Printed by and for William Hone, 67, Old Bailey, three doors from Ludgate Hill. 1817. Price Sixpence.)

OR; B.M. 1200. d. 16. (2.); circa 22 × 14 cm; 16 pp.; 1 plate.

9

ANON – *The life, accouchement, and death of the Princess Charlotte; with her portrait taken from her death-bed. This deeply affecting narrative is fully illustrated by letters, papers and important documents; together with some interesting remarks on the succession to the throne.* All things that we ordained festival Turn from their office to black funeral; Our instruments, to melancholy bells; Our wedding cheer, to a sad burial feast; Our solemn hymns to sullen dirges change; Our bridal flowers serve for a bury'd corse, And all things change them to the contrary!! Shakspeare. (London: Printed and published by Hay and Turner, 11, Newcastle Street, Strand; and may be had of all booksellers in town and country. Price One Shilling.) [1817].

OR; B.M. 1200. d. 31.; circa 22 × 14 cm; 24 pp.; 1 plate.

10

ANON – *The real or moral cause of Her Royal Highness the Princess Charlotte's death, with authentic and interesting particulars of that tragical event. Dedicated to His Serene Highness Prince Leopold.* Second Edition. 'Minatur ne caedat, caedit ne occidat.' (London: Printed for the Author, by R. Clay, Devonshire Street, Bishopsgate; and sold by Burton & Briggs, Leadenhall Street; and Simpkin and Marshall, Stationers' Court. 1817.)

OR; circa 23 × 14.5 cm; xii + 13 to 78 pp. The B.M. Catalogue lists the 1st Edition: 1200. d. 32.

11

ANON – Second Edition, with account of the embalment, funeral preparations, &c. &c. &c. *The virtuous life and lamented death of Her Royal Highness the Princess Charlotte. Including every interesting particular relative to her accouchement, and death!* 'Tis not the sable garb, the room of state, The minute bell that tells the fatal tale; – She, she is gone for whom we felt elate; 'Tis the fond wife, the mother, we bewail, Young, loving and beloved; the good, the great, She was a nation's hope – a nation's pride: With her that pride has fled – those hopes have died. (London: Printed by G. Smeeton, St. Martin's Lane. Price Four-Pence.) [1817].

OR; circa 17 × 11 cm; 20 pp. The B.M. Catalogue lists, under the same title, a pamphlet of 52 pp. with 3 plates: 1202. h. 27. (3.).

12

ANON (Alice Tribe) – *Tributary tears, sacred to the memory of the illustrious and amiable Princess Charlotte of Wales, and Saxe-Coburg; who died November 6, 1817, in the twenty-second year of her age. Being a collection of the best poems that have appeared on the occasion. To which is prefixed, a brief memoir of her life.* Yes, she was good as she was fair, None, none on earth above her; As pure in thought as angels are, To see her, was to love her! Second Edition. (London: Printed by and for R. Edwards, Crane-Court, Fleet-Street. 1818.)

OR; B.M. 11644. aa. 36.; circa 15 × 9.5 cm; xxviii + 220 + 4 unnumbered pp.; 1 plate.

13

ARMITAGE, J. – *The sigh of sympathy, a short poem, occasioned by the much-lamented death of Her Royal Highness the Princess Charlotte of Wales; who expired at half past two o'clock, on Thursday morning, November 6, 1817.* By J. Armitage. To him not e'en a father's joys remain To trace the mother in the infant's mien; O may his God his poignant grief assuage, And free-electing grace his soul engage. May balm from Jesus heal the inveterate wound, And his lov'd Princess with the just be found. (London: Published for the Author, by G. Hebert,

88, Cheapside; and to be had of most booksellers; and printed by T. H. Coe, Little Carter Lane, St. Paul's. 1817.)

OR; B.M. 11641. f. 69. (17.); circa 22 × 14 cm; 7 pp.

14

ASPLAND, Robert – *A funeral sermon, preached on Wednesday, November 19, 1817, the day of the interment of Her late Royal Highness the Princess Charlotte of Wales; before the Unitarian Church, Hackney*. By Robert Aspland, Minister of the Church. The fashion of this world passeth away. 1 Cor. vii. 31. (London: Printed by G. Smallfield, Hackney, for R. Hunter, St. Paul's Church-Yard; and D. Eaton, High Holborn. 1817.)

OR; B.M. 695. g. 17. (1.); circa 21 × 14 cm; 22 pp.

15

BOSCAWEN, M. – *Sketch of the life of Her Royal Highness Princess Charlotte Augusta, consort of His Royal Highness Prince Leopold of Saxe Cobourg: being an attempt to delineate her character and moral worth, with authentic particulars of her indisposition and much lamented death*. By M. Boscawen. Her integrity of character must insure the esteem of all. Whitbread. (London: Printed for Walker and Mason, 1, Creed-Lane, Ludgate Hill.) [1817].

OR; B.M. 1202. h. 27. (6.); circa 19.5 × 12 cm; 36 pp.; 1 plate. Printed by T. Hamblin, Garlick-Hill, Thames-Street.

16

CHAPLIN, William – *A sermon occasioned by the lamented death of the Princess Charlotte Augusta; preached on Wednesday, November 19th, 1817, at Bishops Stortford, Herts*. By William Chaplin, Protestant Dissenting Minister in that town. (Bishops Stortford: Printed and sold by William Thorogood; sold also by T. Sparling, Stortford; and Josiah Conder, St. Paul's Church Yard, London. Price One Shilling.) [1817].

OR; circa 22 × 14 cm; iv + 24 pp.

17

CHURCHILL, James – *The nation in tears. A sermon, occasioned by the deeply-lamented death of Her Royal Highness the Princess Charlotte Augusta; who departed this life early in the morning of the 6th of November, 1817, in the twenty-second year of her age; with interesting allusions to Her Royal Highness and the Prince of Saxe-Cobourg. Preached at Weston-Green Chapel, near Claremont, Nov. 16, 1817, and by desire at Hampton Chapel, on the 19th instant, and at Esher, on the 24th.* By the Rev. James Churchill, Thames Ditton, Surry. 'She hath given up the ghost; her sun is gone down, while it was yet day!' Jer. XV. 9. 'Pallida mors aequo pulsat pede pauperum tabernas 'Regumque turres! O beate Sexti, 'Vitae summa brevis spem nos vetat inchoare longam. 'Jam te premet nox!' Hor. Ode iv. Lib. 1. Fourth Edition, enlarged. (London: Printed for D. Cox, 39, High-Street, Southwark; sold also by Sherwood, Neely, and Jones, Paternoster-Row; Williams, and Simpkin and Marshall, Stationers'-Court; Asperne, Cornhill; Burton and Briggs, Leadenhall-Street; Wilson, Cornhill; Chappell, Cornhill; and Low, Gracechurch-Street. 1817.)

OR; circa 22 × 14 cm; 3 unnumbered and 40 numbered pp.; Printed by Barnard and Farley, Skinner Street, London. The B.M. Catalogue lists the 1st Edition: 10805. e. 23.

18

CLERGYMAN OF THE CHURCH OF ENGLAND, A – *A letter, addressed to His Royal Highness the Prince Regent: occasioned by the death of Her Royal Highness the Princess Charlotte of Wales, &c. &c.* By a Clergyman of the Church of England. (London: Printed for L. B. Seeley, No. 169, Fleet Street. 1818.)

OR; circa 22 × 14 cm; 20 pp. J. Dennett, Printer, Leather Lane, Holborn.

19

COOKE, William – *An address to British females on the moral management of pregnancy and labour, and some cursory observations on medical deportment. Suggested by the death of Her Royal Highness Princess Charlotte Augusta of Wales. With a vindication of Her Royal Highness's Physicians, Sir Richard Croft, Dr. Baillie, and Dr. Sims.* By William Cooke, surgeon-accoucheur. 'To enjoy happiness is a great blessing: – to confer it, a greater.' (London: Printed for E. Cox and Son, St. Thomas's Street, Borough. 1817.)

PH; B.M. 1178. i. 19.; circa 22.5 × 14 cm; iv + 44 pp; J. M'Creery, Printer, Black-Horse-Court, London.

20

FOOT, Jesse – *A letter on the necessity of a public inquiry into the cause of the death of Her Royal Highness the Princess Charlotte and her infant, as it appeared in The Sun newspaper on the 13th, together with some additions.* By Jesse Foot, Esq. (London: Printed for J. Walker, 44, Paternoster Row. 1817.)

PH; B.M. T. 1099. (6.); circa 23 × 14 cm; 16 pp. Printed by J. F. Dove, St. John's-square. (In *The Sun* of Nov. 13 the letter is dated Nov. 11; here it is dated Nov. 18.)

(20a) Id. Second Edition, 1817. PH.

21

FOOT, Jesse – *A second letter on the necessity of a public inquiry into the cause of the death of Her Royal Highness the Princess Charlotte and her infant.* By Jesse Foot, Esq. *As it appeared in The Sun of the 15th instant.* (London: Printed for J. Walker, 44, Paternoster Row. 1817.)

PH; circa 23 × 14 cm; 20 pp. Printed by J. F. Dove, St. John's-square. (In *The Sun* of Dec. 15 the letter is not dated; here it is dated Dec. 22.)

22

GREEN, Thomas – *Memoirs of Her late Royal Highness Charlotte-*

Augusta of Wales, and of Saxe-Cobourg; containing an account of her juvenile years - education - marriage with Prince Leopold - accouchement - death – and funeral. To which is prefixed, a concise history of the illustrious House of Brunswick, brought down to the present time; shewing the actual state of the succession to the Throne of the United Kingdom of Great Britain. By Thomas Green, Esq. 'Loveliness was around her as light. She saw the youth, and loved him. Her blue eyes roll'd on him in secret, and she blest the chief.' 'Thou hast left no son, but thy name shall live in song. Narrow is thy dwelling now, thou who wert so great before.' Ossian. (Caxton Press: Printed by Nuttall, Fischer, and Dixon, Liverpool, printers in ordinary to His Majesty. Sold at their Warehouse, 87, Bartholomew Close, London; and by the booksellers of the United Kingdom.) [1818].

OR; B.M. 610. i. 8.; circa 23 × 14 cm; viii + 9 to 576 pp., preceded by an illustrated frontispiece; 11 plates.

23

HAMILTON, Edwin B. – *A record of the life and death of Her Royal Highness the Princess Charlotte.* By Edwin B. Hamilton, Esq. 'I'd ever watch her mouldering clay, And pray for her eternal rest; When time had worn her form away, Her dust I'd place within my breast.' (London: Printed for J. Bumpus, No. 6, Holborn Bars. 1817.)

OR; B.M. 10806. a. 49. (1.); circa 16 × 10 cm; viii + 160 pp.; 2 plates. J. M'Creery, Printer, Black-Horse-Court, London.

(23a) Id., Second Edition, 1817. OR.

24

HOOPER, Mrs. B. – *A poem occasioned by the cessation of public mourning for Her Royal Highness the Princess Charlotte; together with sonnets and other productions.* By Mrs. B. Hooper. (London: Printed for the Author, and sold by Messrs. Suttaby, Evance, and Fox, Stationers' Court; and all other booksellers. 1818.)

OR; circa 17.5 × 11 cm; xi + 143 pp. C. Baldwin, Printer, New Bridge-Street, London.

25

HUISH, Robert – *Memoirs of Her late Royal Highness Charlotte Augusta, Princess of Wales, &c. (from infancy to the period of her much lamented death, funeral rites, &c. &c.) and of her illustrious consort Prince Leopold of Saxe-Coburg Saalfeld; including a variety of anecdotes, hitherto unpublished, with specimens of Her Royal Highness' compositions in prose, poetry, and music, and fac-similes of her hand-writing; comprising also an historical memoir of the House of Saxe-Coburg Saalfeld. The whole collected and arranged, from authorized sources only,* By Robert Huish, Esq. author of 'The Peruvians', &c. &c. Quis talia fando Myrmidonum Dolophumve aut duri miles Ulyssei Temperet à lachrymis? Virg. Ornamented with interesting engravings. (London: Printed for Thomas Kelly, Paternoster-Row. 1818.)

Followed by:

A sacred memorial of Her late Royal Highness Charlotte Augusta, Princess of Wales, and of Saxe-Coburg Saalfeld; being extracts from upwards of one hundred and twenty sermons, preached on the day of her interment, by the most eminent divines of all denominations. Selected by Robert Huish, Esq. and forming a supplement to his 'Memoirs of the Princess Charlotte,' &c. (London: Printed for Thomas Kelly, 53, Paternoster-Row, by W. Clowes, Northumberland-Court, Strand. 1818.)

OR; B.M. 610. i. 9. (1.) and (2).; circa 22 × 14 cm; illustrated frontispiece, title, ii + xv + 696 pp.; 10 plates. 'A sacred memorial': illustrated frontispiece, viii + 136 pp.

(25a) Id.: A new edition, revised, augmented, and improved. 1821. 'A sacred memorial' is dated 1819. OR.

26

IVIMEY, Joseph – *Reasons why the Protestant Dissenters lament the death of Her Royal Highness the Princess Charlotte Augusta, the illustrious consort of His Serene Highness Prince Leopold, of Saxe-Cobourg, and daughter of His Royal Highness the Prince Regent, who died at Claremont, Nov. 6, 1817; aged 22. A sermon preached at the Baptist Meeting, Eagle Street, London, on Nov. 19, the day of the funeral at Windsor.* By Joseph Ivimey. 'Death is come up into our windows, and is entered into our palaces.' 'Her sun is gone down while it was yet day.' (London: Printed by Arding and Merrett, 21, Old Boswell Court, Carey Street: sold by Button and Son, Paternoster Row; Kent, Holborn; Williams, Stationers' Court; and Arding, 71, Fetter Lane, Holborn.) [1818?].

OR; B.M. 10805. d. 23. (15.); circa 22 × 14 cm; 34 pp. The B.M. Catalogue also lists an edition dated 1817, with the words 'in particular' between 'Dissenters' and 'lament': 10806. cc. 26.

27

M'I., D. – *The life of the late Princess Charlotte; detailing her birth, education and sweet disposition, while an infant – Her progress in learning and polite accomplishments – With many interesting stories of Her Royal Highness during that period. – Her attachment to religious duties, and her charitable demeanour to relieve the distresses of the indigent – The addresses of the Hereditary Prince of Orange – The reluctance of the Princess to quit England, or to give her hand without the most cordial approbation of her heart – The filial reverence which she always manifested towards both her Royal Parents – Prince Leopold's first introduction to her – His amiable demeanour attracts her notice, and impresses her mind with favourable sentiments towards him – The honourable and manly conduct of Prince Leopold as soon as he perceived the indications of her esteem – His frank declaration to the Prince Regent – The Regent's free consent – The genealogy of Prince Leopold, with some account of his life – The nuptial ceremony – Their abode at Claremont – The affectionate, exemplary and domestic way in which their time was passed, and the charitable actions of both – Symptoms of Her Royal Highness's pregnancy – Her accouchement, and her ever lamentable end – The funeral, etc. etc.* (London: Printed for, and published by T. Kinnersley, 3, Acton Place, Kingsland Road. 1818.)

OR; B.M. 10805. dd. 3.; circa 22 × 14 cm; illustrated frontispiece + iv + 596 pp.; 10 plates. Stereotyped and printed by J. M'Gowan, 16, Great Windmill Street, Haymarket.

28

PHILLIPS, Charles – *The lament of the Emerald Isle.* By Charles Phillips, Esq. 'Loveliness was around her as light. She saw the youth, and loved him. Her blue eye rolled on him in secret, and she blessed the chief of Morven – 'Thou has left no son, but thy name shall live in song; – 'Narrow is thy dwelling now, thou who wert so great before.' Ossian – Songs of Selma. Sixth Edition – with additions. (London: Printed for William Hone, 67, Old Bailey, three doors from Ludgate-Hill. 1818.)

OR; B.M. 11662. ee. 9.; circa 22 × 14 cm; x + 11 to 22 pp.; J. M'Creery, Printer, Black-Horse-Court, London. The B.M. Catalogue also lists the 1st and 2nd Editions, 1817: 11641. f. 69. (8.) and 09525. l. 33. (22.).

29

PRICE, Rees – *A critical inquiry into the nature and treatment of the case of Her Royal Highness the Princess Charlotte of Wales and her infant son, with the probable causes of their deaths, and the subsequent appearances. The whole fully discussed, and illustrated by comparative practice; pointing out the means of preventing such evils in future; particularly worthy the attention of the Faculty and the Public. Respectfully dedicated to the Imperial Parliament of the United Kingdom of Great Britain.* 'Hence 'tis we wait the wond'rous cause to find.' By Rees Price, Member of the Royal College of Surgeons, London. (London: Printed for the Author; and sold by C. Chapple, 66, Pall-Mall; J. Asperne, 32, Cornhill; and all booksellers in the United Kingdom. 1817. Price Three Shillings and Sixpence.)

PH; circa 22 × 14 cm; xvi + 17 to 64 pp.; W. Pople, Printer, 67, Chancery Lane. The B.M. Catalogue lists it as missing.

30

READ, William – *An effusion of feeling on the lamented death of the Princess Charlotte of Wales.* By William Read, Esq. 'So, through the cloud of death, her spirit passed Into that pure and unknown world of love, Where injury cannot come: – and here is laid The mortal body by her infant's side.' Wordsworth. (London: Printed for Henry Colburn, Conduit Street. 1817.)

OR; circa 22 × 14 cm; 7 pp. Printed by Cox and Baylis, Great Queen Street, Lincoln's-Inn Fields.

31

SCOTO-BRITANNUS (Thomas MacCrie) – *Free thoughts on the late religious celebration of the funeral of Her Royal Highness the Princess Charlotte of Wales; and on the discussion to which it has given rise in Edinburgh.* By Scoto-Britannus. Non civium ardor prava jubentium Mente quatit solida. – Hor. (Edinburgh: Printed for MacRedie, Skelly, and Company, 52. Prince's-Street. 1817.)

OR; B.M. 10806. c. 20.; circa 22 × 14 cm; title + 78 pp. Printed by Walker and Greig, Edinburgh.

32

TAYLOR, George – *The flower of Brunswick, an elegy*; By George Taylor, author of 'The spirit of the mountains', &c. &c. 'O eloquent, just, and mighty death, whom none could advise, thou hast persuaded; what none hath dared, thou hast done; and whom all the world hath flattered, thou only hast cast out of the world.' Sir Walter Raleigh. Death lays his icy hand on kings; Sceptre and crown Must tumble down, – And in the dust be equal made, With the poor crooked scythe and spade. James Shirley. (London: Printed for Donald MacKay, 44, Newgate Street. 1817.)

OR; circa 22 × 14 cm; 11 pp. Printed by Kaygill & Rowe, Newgate-Street.

33

THOMSON, Anthony Todd – *The authentic medical statement of the case of Her Royal Highness the late Princess Charlotte of Wales; extracted from the forty-eighth number of the 'London Medical Repository;' published 1st December, 1817. Edited by G. M. Burrows, M.D., F.L.S. &c., and Mr. A. T. Thomson, with some prefatory and concluding observations.* By Anthony Todd Thomson, F.L.S. Member of the Royal College of Surgeons, &c. 'The heart that glowed with the purest fire, and beat with the best affections, is now become a clod of the valley.' Logan's Sermons. (London: Sold by Longman, Hurst, Rees, Orme, and Brown, No. 39, Paternoster Row; and by all the booksellers in the United Kingdom.) [1818?].

PH; B.M. T. 1099. (5.); circa 22 × 14 cm; 36 pp. Printed by J. Brettell, Rupert Street, Haymarket, London.

Notes

[1] Oil on canvas, 102 × 81 cm (Kenneth Garlick, *Sir Thomas Lawrence*, Boston Book & Art Shop, 1955, p. 32, No. 3, and Plate 91).

Princess Charlotte sat at Claremont to Sir Thomas Lawrence in the autumn of 1817, as she wished to make a present of this portrait to Prince Leopold on his 27th birthday (16 December 1817). In her *Recollections of Sir Thomas Lawrence, P.R.A., during an intimacy of nearly thirty years* (Appendix to G. S. Layard's *Sir Thomas Lawrence's letter-bag*, G. Allen, London 1906, p. 276) Miss Elizabeth Croft (1769–1856), Sir Richard's half-sister, wrote: 'Immediately upon her death the Regent sent for her portrait to Carlton House, not aware that she intended it for Prince Leopold, this intention being confided to Sir Thomas, whom she commanded to complete it for the Prince's birthday. Sir Thos. was greatly distressed by the Regent's refusal to give it up; so very awkward was his situation, that he was obliged to go to Brighton to explain, and intercede for it; and I understood that the difficulty was very great, and only overcome by bribing the Regent with the promise of an excellent whole-length copy, which is now in the collection of the present King William the 4th'. (In his book *The later Georgian Pictures in the collection of Her Majesty the Queen*, Phaidon Press Ltd., London 1969, vol. I, pp. 79–80, No. 925, Oliver Millar lists only one half-length copy which he supposes to have been made for Queen Victoria in 1870.)

Sir Thomas Lawrence brought the portrait himself to Prince Leopold on 16 December. (*v.* G. S. Layard, *loc. cit.*, pp. 109–113; D. E. Williams, *The life and correspondence of Sir Thomas Lawrence*, H. Colburn & R. Bentley, London 1831, vol. II, pp. 80–85; *The Farington Diary*, by Joseph Farington, R.A. [1747–1821], Ed. by James Greig, Hutchinson & Co., London 1928, vol. VIII, pp. 140–161, *passim.*) On 14 November 1817 Sir Thomas had written: 'My Picture is at Carleton House – Are you not glad that it was painted? It is (for *here* I will speak as a Stranger) the only One that will properly represent to the People of England, the sweet beneficent Monarch they have lost!' (Postscript to letter LAW/9/15, to

Miss Elizabeth Croft. Property of The National Trust, Croft Castle, Leominster, Herefs.)

[2] Her titles were proclaimed at her funeral by Garter Principal King of Arms: 'The Most Illustrious Princess Charlotte Augusta, Daughter of His Royal Highness George Prince of Wales, Regent of this United Kingdom; Consort of His Serene Highness Leopold George Frederick, Duke of Saxe, Margrave of Misnia, Landgrave of Thuringia, Prince of Coburg of Saalfeld; and Granddaughter of His Most Excellent Majesty George the Third, by the Grace of God of the United Kingdom of Great Britain and Ireland King, Defender of the Faith.'

She was habitually styled Princess Charlotte of Wales, but was not Princess of Wales, as she is sometimes referred to, e.g. by Huish (*v*. No. 25, p. 57).

[3] The Princess of Wales's mother, Princess Augusta, Consort of Charles William Ferdinand, Duke of Brunswick-Wolfenbüttel, was a sister of the Prince's father, King George III. There was additional consanguinity, because the King and the Duke were second cousins, the Duke's maternal grandmother, Sophia Dorothea, Queen of Prussia, being the sister of King George II; she and her Consort, King Frederick William I, were first cousins, his mother Sophia Charlotte, Queen of Prussia, Consort of King Frederick I, being the sister of King George I. Both the Prince and the Princess of Wales belonged to the House of Guelph (Welf) and had another common ancestor in Ernest the Confessor (d. 1546), Duke of Lüneburg, great-grandfather of Ernest Augustus, Elector of Hanover (father of George I) and of Ferdinand Albert, whose son Ferdinand Albert II inherited Wolfenbüttel and was the great-grandfather of the Princess.

[4] Dr. Matthew Baillie (Shotts, Lanark., 27 October 1761 – Duntisbourne Abbots, Glos., 23 September 1823). His mother Dorothea was sister of Dr. William and Mr. John Hunter. Lecturer on Anatomy in his uncle William's School in Great Windmill Street, Haymarket, 1781–1799. B.A., M.A., M.B., M.D. (Oxford 1783, 1786, 1786 and 1789). Physician to St. George's Hospital 1787–1799. Candidate of the R.C.P. of London in 1789, Fellow in

1790, Censor in 1791 and 1796, Elect in 1809. On 5 May 1791 married Sophia Denman (1771–1845), the younger of the twin daughters of Dr. Thomas Denman (1733–1815), the celebrated man-midwife. Fellow of the Royal Societies of London and of Edinburgh. One of the Trustees of the Medical and Chirurgical Society of London, many times Member of its Council, President in 1808 and 1809. Honorary Member of the R.C.P. of Edinburgh and of the Medical Societies of Erlangen and of Bonn. Physician Extraordinary to King George III in 1810. Appointed Physician-in-Ordinary to Princess Charlotte on 22 July 1816 (Hunter Baillie Collection [27], vol. VII, p. 46). The last possessor of 'the gold-headed cane' (now at the R.C.P. of London), the former owners having been Dr. John Radcliffe (1650–1714), Dr. Richard Mead (1673–1754), Dr. Anthony Askew (1722–1774), Dr. William Pitcairn (1711–1791) and Dr. David Pitcairn (1749–1809). Outstanding among his contributions to medical literature is *The morbid anatomy of some of the most important parts of the human body* (J. Johnson & G. Nicol, London 1793, and many later editions and translations), the first systematic treatise on the subject. (G. B. Morgagni's pioneer work *De sedibus, et causis morborum per anatomen indagatis*, Venice 1761, is a collection of cases and necropsies.)

Dr. Baillie is commemorated in Westminster Abbey, Chapel of St. Andrew, by a bust and an inscription.

[5] Sir Richard Croft, Bart. (London, 9 January 1762–London, 13 February 1818). Descended from a very ancient and distinguished family in Herefordshire; Croft Castle, near Leominster, was in its possession before the Norman Conquest. Chirurgus privilegiatus (Oxford 1788). On 3 November 1789 married Margaret Denman (1771–1847), the elder of the twin daughters of Dr. Thomas Denman. Attended in Passy (Paris), in 1790, Georgiana, Duchess of Devonshire, when she gave birth to the 6th Duke. M.D. (Aberdeen 1792). For many years one of the leading accoucheurs in London. Physician-Accoucheur to the Lying-in Charity for Delivering Poor Married Women at their own Habitations. Member of the Medical and Chirurgical Society of London. Appointed Surgeon-in-Ordinary to Princess Charlotte and Prince Leopold on 3 November 1817 (*v.* II). Succeeded to the Baronetcy, as 6th Baronet, on 26 April 1816, on the death of his brother, the Rev. Sir Herbert Croft, B.C.L.,

Vicar of Prittlewell, Essex, the well known literary man, bibliophile and linguist.

[6] Dr. John Sims (Canterbury, Kent, 13 October 1749 – Dorking, Surrey, 26 February 1831). M.D. (Edinburgh 1774). Licentiate of the R.C.P. of London in 1779. Physician to the Surrey Dispensary. Consulting Physician-Accoucheur to the Lying-in Charity for Delivering Poor Married Women at their own Habitations. Consulting Physician to the Royal Ear Dispensary. Member of the Medical and Chirurgical Society of London. Fellow and one-time President (1783) of the Medical Society of London, Member of the Society's Midwifery Committee. Member of the Society of Physicians and of the Society for the Improvement of Medical Knowledge. Editor of Curtis's *Botanical Magazine* and of the *Annals of Botany*. Fellow of the Linnaean Society and of the Royal Society.

Princess Charlotte's Consultant Accoucheur is sometimes confused with his homonymous relative Dr. John Sims (1792–1838), M.D. (Edinburgh 1818), Licentiate of the R.C.P. of London in 1819, Physician to the Marylebone Infirmary, and, because their names have the same initial J., with Dr. James Sims (1741–1820), M.D. (Leyden 1764), Licentiate of the R.C.P. of London in 1778, Physician to the General Dispensary.

[7] Black and red chalk, 38 × 26 cm (No. 79 in the Catalogue of Sir Thomas Lawrence's Exhibition, Royal Academy of Arts Diploma Gallery, London 1961). Miss Elizabeth Croft (*loc. cit.*, pp. 244–245, *v.* Note 1) wrote: 'I had proofs of his [Sir Thomas Lawrence's] desire to oblige and gratify me by his making a drawing of my nephew Herbert Ryder . . . in 1810, and another of my dear Brother about the same period, which, though never finished, is a striking likeness of that bright and benevolent being whom he afterwards delineated under circumstances the most melancholy. In 1818 he made a drawing of my brother in his coffin, and by his magical power contrived to give it the appearance of sleep in his armchair. I am certain he considered it one of his most exquisite performances, as he constantly sent for it when he had artists dining with him. One friend called it 'the triumph of Genius over death', and Sir David Wilkie said it was 'absolutely sublime, and worthy of the pencil of Michael Angelo'.

In a note among the Croft family papers it is written that Sir Thomas spent twelve hours altogether in the room with the body of Sir Richard. Miss Croft, to whom he gave the pastel, put it in a wooden case under lock and key. When she died, in 1856, she left it to Sir Archer Denman Croft (1801–1865), the 8th Baronet, who was at that time the eldest surviving son of Sir Richard. (Herbert had died in 1802, when 9 years old; Richard Denman in 1798, in the second year of his age; Sir Thomas Elmsley, the 7th Baronet, in 1835, when 37 years old; Joseph Denman in 1804, as an infant.) Sir Archer refused to have it or to have the subject mentioned to him. It was accordingly given to the youngest son, the Rev. Richard Croft (1808–1869). The present owner, R. Page Croft, Esq., his great-grandson, also possesses the 1810 drawing (No. 60 in the same Catalogue).

The daughter of Arthur Keightley (the friend and executor of Sir Thomas Lawrence) made a copy of the post-mortem drawing with Sir Thomas Lawrence's own chalks, lent for the purpose. This copy is owned by the present Lord Croft, another great-grandson of the Rev. Richard Croft.

According to a report of the time Sir Richard had shot himself with two pistols, 'one . . . loaded with slugs, the other with ball. Both were discharged and the head of the unfortunate gentleman literally blown to pieces.' The ball seems to have lodged itself from behind into the frontal bone, above the left eyebrow; no effect of the slugs is visible in the drawing.

[8] Holland, Sir Eardley – 'The Princess Charlotte of Wales: a triple obstetric tragedy.' *The Journal of Obstetrics & Gynaecology of the British Empire*, **58,** No. 6, 905–919, December 1951.

[9] Thomas Denman (1779–1854), only son of Dr. Thomas Denman and brother of Lady Croft and Mrs. Baillie. M.P. 1819–1826 and 1830–1832. Princess Charlotte's mother, Queen Caroline, appointed him her Solicitor-general, and he was one of the defending Counsel at her trial before the House of Lords in 1820. Common Serjeant of the City of London 1822–1830; Attorney General 1830–1832; Lord Chief Justice 1832–1850. Created Baron Denman of Dovedale in 1834.

[10] It is difficult to say how long Princess Charlotte's labour was overdue. According to III, 3, §1, 3 November was 'forty two weeks & one day from her last recovery' (12 January); according to III, 4, §1, 3 November was 'forty two Weeks & two days, from H.R.H's

earliest reckoning' (11 January). In her letter of 14 March (I, 1, §1) the Princess had written: 'the 2^d *period* is now *Safely past over A week*'; therefore the last one should have been before 7 January. On 19 October Sir Richard Croft wrote from Claremont to his half-sister, Miss Elizabeth Croft: 'This is the first day I could by reason expect H.R.H. to be put to Bed' (G. S. Layard, *loc. cit.*, p. 114, *v.* Note 1).

[11] The Dowager Countess, one of the Queen's Ladies of the Bedchamber. Elizabeth (1758–1823), daughter of John Waldegrave, 3rd Earl Waldegrave, had married in 1791, as his second wife, James Brudenell, 5th Earl of Cardigan, who died in 1811.

[12] Mrs. Griffiths was at the Princess's bedside when H.R.H. began to feel ill after her labour; in the reports of the time she is styled 'the nurse'. Mrs. Jans was obviously a candidate for appointment as wet nurse; so far I have found no further mention of her nor of Mrs. Winchester.

[13] Sir Robert William Gardiner (1781–1864), principal Equerry to Prince Leopold from the Prince's marriage until he became King of the Belgians. Brevet-lieutenant-colonel Royal Horse Artillery 1812–1831. K.C.B. 1814. Had served on the continent from 1797 to 1815, when he commanded his troops through the Waterloo campaign and entered Paris. Governor and Commander-in-Chief at Gibraltar, 1848–1855. Colonel-Commandant R.H.A. 1853, General 1854. Died at Melbourne Lodge, Claremont.

[14] The Prelates and Ministers who were summoned for the birth of the Royal Infant: Charles Manners Sutton, Archbishop of Canterbury; William Howley, Bishop of London; John Scott, 1st Baron Eldon (1st Viscount Encombe and 1st Earl of Eldon, 1821), Lord Chancellor; Henry Addington, 1st Viscount Sidmouth, Secretary of the Home Department; Henry Bathurst, 3rd Earl Bathurst, Minister for War and Colonies; Nicholas Vansittart (1st Baron Bexley, 1823), Chancellor of the Exchequer.

[15] Acute dilatation of the stomach may be rapidly fatal. Nobody has pointed out, as far as I know, this possible cause of Princess Charlotte's death, but Dr. Alexander Morison noted in 1917: 'Death

under the circumstances seems to have been attributable less to the quantity of blood lost . . . than to the diastolic atony of the viscera. The stomach of the Princess is also stated to have contained *three pints* of fluid, which is . . . evidence of . . . concord both in tone and in atony in the viscera post partum, influenced by the common nervous system. . . . Some of this gastric fluid was doubtless introduced in the agonised efforts at rescue, the organ being too atonic either to reject or propel it. A satisfactory vomit under the circumstances is frequently associated with an immediate increase of both cardiac and uterine tone.' ('Sir Richard Croft and the case of the Princess Charlotte', Letter dated 1 December 1917, to the Editor of *The Lancet*, **2**, 874, No. 4919, 8 December 1917).

Alexander [Blackhall-]Morison (1850–1927), M.D., Fellow of the R.C.P. of Edinburgh and of London, member of the staffs of several London hospitals, Physician in charge of heart cases at the Mount Vernon Hospital, was the grandson of Sir Alexander Morison (1779–1866), M.D., Fellow of the R.C.P. of Edinburgh and of London, Inspecting Physician of Lunatic Asylums in Surrey, Physician to Bethlehem Hospital, who had been appointed Physician Extraordinary to Princess Charlotte and Prince Leopold in 1816.

[16] Sir David Dundas, Bart. (?–1826). Member of the Surgeons Company in 1777. Practised mostly as an apothecary in Richmond, Surrey. Appointed Sergeant-Surgeon to King George III in 1793. Member of the Court of Assistants and of the Court of Examiners of the R.C.S. in 1800. Master of the College in 1804, 1811 and 1819. Created a Baronet in 1815.

[17] Sir Everard Home, Bart. (1756–1832). Fellow of the Royal Society in 1785. Member of the Court of Assistants of the R.C.S. in 1801, of the Court of Examiners in 1809. Master of the College in 1813, President in 1821. Appointed Sergeant-Surgeon to King George III in 1808. Created a Baronet in 1813. Surgeon to St. George's Hospital 1793–1827, to the Royal Hospital, Chelsea, from 1821. He was a relative of Dr. Baillie, his sister Anne having married Mr. John Hunter, Dr. Baillie's maternal uncle. One of the official duties of the Sergeant-Surgeons was to embalm the bodies of members of the Royal Family.

[18] Sir Benjamin Bloomfield (1768–1846). Private Secretary to

the Prince Regent. Lieutenant-General and Colonel-Commandant Royal Horse Artillery. M.P. 1812–1818. Knighted in 1815. Appointed Minister Plenipotentiary to the Court of Stockholm in 1822. Raised to the Irish Peerage in 1825, as Baron Bloomfield of Oakhampton and Redwood, Tipperary.

Sir B. Bloomfield's letter was published in *The Sun* of Friday, 14 November (from *The Morning Post*).

[19] Lady Georgiana Dorothy (1783–1858), elder daughter of William Cavendish, 5th Duke of Devonshire, married in 1801 George Howard (1773–1848), Lord Morpeth, who succeeded his father as 6th Earl of Carlisle in 1825. Richard Croft had been in Passy in 1790 to attend her mother, Georgiana, Duchess of Devonshire, for her third confinement (when the 6th Duke was born) and had then also attended the 7-year-old Lady Georgiana in a dangerous illness. Castle Howard, in Yorkshire, was the seat of the Earls of Carlisle.

[20] Colonel James Bathurst (1782–1850), later General Sir James Bathurst, K.C.B., had been A.D.C., A.Q.M.G., to the Duke of Wellington in the Peninsula. Second cousin of the 3rd Earl Bathurst [14]. In 1815 he had married Lady Caroline, daughter of Andrew Thomas Stewart-Moore Stuart, 1st Earl Castle Stewart. Their third child was born in March 1818, a few weeks after Sir Richard's suicide.

[21] Mrs. Campbell, Sub-Governess to the Princess in 1805–1806 and from 1814 to 1816; Bed-chamber Woman and Holder of the Privy Purse after the Princess's marriage.

[22] Sir William Knighton, Bart. (1776–1836), M.D. (Aberdeen 1806), one of the Prince Regent's Physicians. Licentiate of the R.C.P. in 1806. Auditor of the Duchies of Cornwall and Lancaster. Created a Baronet in 1812. In 1822 he succeeded Sir Benjamin Bloomfield [18] as Private Secretary and Keeper of the Privy Purse to King George IV.

[23] Princess Mary (1776–1856), eleventh child and fourth daughter of King George III, Princess Charlotte's aunt, had married on 22 July 1816 her first cousin William Frederick, Duke of Gloucester.

[24] Lady Anne Culling Smith (1768–1844), the Duchess of York's Lady-in-Waiting, was daughter of Garrett Wellesley, 2nd Baron Mornington, 1st Viscount Wellesley and 1st Earl of Mornington, and sister of the Duke of Wellington. In 1790 she had married the Hon. Henry FitzRoy (fourth son of Charles, 1st Baron Southampton), who died in 1794, and in 1799 she married Charles Culling Smith of Hampton, Under Secretary of State, Foreign Department, 1809–1812. In 1814 her daughter Georgiana Frederica FitzRoy married Henry Somerset, Marquess of Worcester, who succeeded his father in 1835 as 7th Duke of Beaufort; she died in 1821 and the Marquess married her half-sister, Emily Frances Culling Smith, in 1822.

[25] The Dowager Countess. Frances (1753–1821), only daughter of the Rt. Rev. Philip Twysden, D.D., Bishop of Raphoe, Ireland, in 1770 had married George Bussy Villiers, 4th Earl of Jersey (1735–1805). She was the Prince of Wales's reputed mistress at the time of his marriage to Princess Caroline.

[26] Christian Friedrich Stockmar (Coburg, Bavaria, 22 August 1787 – Coburg, 9 July 1863). M.D. (Würzburg ? 1810); Prince Leopold's physician. In 1821 he received a patent of Saxon nobility, in 1830 was raised to the rank of Baron (Freiherr von Stockmar) in Bavaria and in 1844 in Austria. Confidential adviser to Prince Leopold, Queen Victoria and the Prince Consort.

Although residing at Claremont he did not have any share in the management of the Princess and only saw her when she was dying. In his Diary he wrote: 'She was in a state of great suffering and disquiet from spasms in her chest and difficulty in breathing, tossed about incessantly from one side to the other, speaking now to Baillie, now to Croft. Baillie said to her, 'Here comes an old friend of yours'. She stretched out her left hand eagerly to me, and pressed mine twice vehemently. I felt her pulse, which was very quick; the beats now full, now weak, now intermittent. Baillie kept giving her wine constantly. She said to me, 'They have made me tipsy'. For about a quarter of an hour I went in and out of the room, then the rattle in the throat began. I had just left the room when she called out loudly, 'Stocky! Stocky!' I went back; she was quieter, but the rattle continued. She turned more than once over on her face, drew her legs up, and her hands grew cold. At two o'clock . . . she was no more.' (*Memoirs of Baron Stockmar. By his son Baron E. von*

Stockmar. Translated from the German by G.A.M. Edited by F. Max Müller. Longmans, Green, and Co., London 1872, Vol. I, pp. 64–65.)

[27] Dr. Matthew Baillie's second and only surviving son (1797–1894) was named William Hunter after his father's maternal uncle and benefactor. His children were styled Hunter Baillie. Out of the ten volumes of documents of the Baillie family at the R.C.S., five were bequeathed by William Hunter Baillie and five presented to the College in 1926 by his daughter, Helen Hunter Baillie. Hence the name given to the Collection.

[28] Ernst Friedrich Herbert, Graf von Münster, Freiherr von Grothaus (1766–1839), had been Hanoverian Minister of State in London since 1805. In 1812 was appointed one of the three Commissioners for the protection and management of the King's private property. Represented Hanover at the Congress of Vienna in 1814–1815, when the Electorate became a Kingdom.

[29] Sudbourne Hall (later demolished), a country seat of Francis Ingram-Seymour Conway, 2nd Marquess of Hertford (1743–1822), Lord Chamberlain of the Household. His second wife, Isabella Anne Ingram Shepherd (1760–1836), first daughter and coheiress of Charles, 9th and last Viscount Irvine, whom the Marquess had married in 1776, was the Prince Regent's reputed mistress.

[30] Princess Charlotte, had she survived, would have become Queen of Great Britain and Ireland in 1830, on the death of her father, King George IV. In accordance with the Salic Law, however, the crown of Hanover would have devolved to one of her uncles and to his male heirs. Count Münster could not have foreseen that exactly the same thing was to happen in 1837, on the death of King William IV. Queen Victoria's Consort was another member of the House of Saxe.

[31] From her note at the end of No. 2 it is obvious that Mrs. Baillie compiled her Notebook after the death of her husband (23 September 1823), copying some of the papers left by him. Text and headings are in her own handwriting. I have added only the numeration and, in square brackets, the names of the senders of the letters.

[32] Dr. Baillie, Sir Richard Croft and Dr. Sims wrote several copies of 'the general statement' (*v.* IV, 5, §4, and 9, §5). Only one is known to survive (Royal Archives, Windsor Castle, Georgian Papers No. 50067/8, endorsed as 'Doctors' Report'). It is written on the four sides of a single quarto sheet of paper folded in two. The statement (No. 50067), in Dr. Baillie's handwriting, begins at the top of the first page, without any heading, ends on the third page (Plate III) and is followed by Dr. Sims's postscript (No. 50068), in his own handwriting, which ends on the fourth and last page with his signature.

Both the statement and the postscript have been published by Lawrence Dopson ('The Bicentenary of John Sims, M.D., F.R.S.', *The Practitioner*, **164**, 156–170, February 1950).

Between the Windsor statement and its only two known copies, published here (VII, 2), there are some irrelevant grammatical differences (spelling, punctuation, abbreviations, use of pronouns instead of nouns and of small and capital letters, etc.). In the Windsor statement the afterbirth is said to have been taken away 'about' twenty minutes before ten, instead of 'at' (§4). There is 'from Her Stomach' between 'threw up' and 'a little fluid' (§5) and 'somewhat' between 'to talk' and 'too much' (§5). There is 'some' instead of 'the' Camphor mixture (§5) and 'breathed' instead of 'began to breathe' (§6). The sentence from 'but there was no reason' until 'danger' (§6) is lacking, as is the 8th and last paragraph.

Dopson's transcription differs from the Windsor statement only in the omission of 'very' between 'this' and 'tedious labour' (§3). 'Probably' instead of 'probable' (§7) must be a misprint (in the Windsor statement Dr. Baillie forgot the middle syllable; one line ends with 'pro-' and the next one begins with 'ble' (Plate III).

Dopson's transcription of Dr. Sims's postscript is quite accurate. The copy made by Sir Richard Croft, published here (III, 7), presents some slight differences which do not alter its meaning. I only mention 'state & progress' of the labour instead of 'state', and 'necessary' instead of 'advisable' (§2). In the endorsement Sir Richard wrote that the statement had been signed by Dr. Baillie and himself; the Windsor statement was also signed by Dr. Sims (Plate III).

Sir Eardley Holland (pp. 908–909) [8] wrote: 'The R.C.S. copy ... is headed "Dr. Baillie's account of Princess Charlotte's labour".' Neither of the R.C.S. copies bears such a heading and no other has been found.

feeble and irregular, and She became extremely restless, not being able to remain a single mo ment in the same posture — This very alarming state continued and kept encreasing till half past Two in the morning, when Her Royal Highness expired — Her mind was entire throughout the whole of this dreadful attack —

The Child had been born dead, but appear ed not to have been dead long — The most strenuous efforts were made to reanimate it by means which had been previously provided, but they were unavailing — Some circumstances had render'd it pro ble that the Child would be Still-born, and therefore every means of recovery were in readiness.

Novr 9 — 1817

M Baillie
Richard Croft.
Jn. Sims

As some of the above circumstances could not come under my immediate observation, not having seen her Royal Highness till symptoms of danger occurred, I beg leave to add, that on my arrival at Claremont,

PLATE III. The third page of the "Doctors' Report" on Princess Charlotte Augusta's labour and death (Royal Archives, Windsor Castle) [32].

[33] It is a footnote in his Autobiography, entitled 'A short memoir of my life, with a view of furnishing authentic materials', edited by James Blake Bailey (*The Practitioner*, O.S. **57**, N.S. **4**, 51–65, 1896).

The sentences copied by Mrs. Baillie are preceded by 'I can never forget the most afflicting scene which I witness'd at Claremont in November, 1817, which not only covered this country with mourning, but filled it with real sorrow of heart' and followed by 'It is not unusual for labours to have been much more protracted and yet to do well by the native efforts of the constitution; and if instruments had been used with the same fatal event, what blame would have been attach'd to him [Sir Richard Croft] from one end of the Kingdom to the other?'

[34] Henry Ainslie (1760–1834), M.D. (Cambridge 1793). Candidate of the R.C.P. in 1794, Fellow in 1795, Censor in 1795, 1803, 1810, 1814 and 1818, Elect in 1818.

[35] William George Maton (1774–1835), M.D. (Oxford 1801). Candidate of the R.C.P. in 1801, Fellow in 1802, Censor in 1804, 1813 and 1824, Elect in 1828. Physician Extraordinary to Queen Charlotte in 1816. Attended the Duke of Kent at Sidmouth in his fatal illness in January 1820 and was appointed Physician-in-Ordinary to the Duchess of Kent and her infant, Princess Alexandrina Victoria.

[36] Pelham Warren (1778–1835), M.D. (Cambridge 1805). Candidate of the R.C.P. in 1805, Fellow in 1806, Censor in 1810, Elect in 1829.

[37] Sir Henry Holland, Bart. (1788–1873), M.D. (Edinburgh 1811). In 1814 Medical Attendant to the Princess of Wales on the continent. F.R.S. in 1816. Licentiate of the R.C.P. in 1816, Fellow in 1828, Censor in 1832, 1836 and 1842, Consiliarius in 1836, 1839, 1844, 1845, 1846, 1850, 1851, 1852 and 1869. Witness at Queen Caroline's trial before the House of Lords in 1820. Physician Extraordinary to King William IV in 1835 and to Queen Victoria in 1837. Physician-in-Ordinary to the Prince Consort in 1840, to the Queen in 1852. Created a Baronet in 1853.

[38] Dr. Sims's letter was published thirty-two years later by

Robert Collins in his book *A short sketch of the life and writings of the late Joseph Clarke, Esq., M.D., Vice-President of the Royal Irish Academy, and formerly Master of the Dublin Lying-in Hospital, etc., etc.* (Longman, Brown, Green, and Longmans, London 1849, pp. 68–70). The letter was printed again twice in the same year: in Robert Lee's paper 'Observations on the cause of death after delivery in the case of Her Royal Highness the Princess Charlotte of Wales' (*The Lancet*, **1**, 450–452, 28 April 1849) and in Charles Clay's periodical *The British Record of Obstetric Medicine and Surgery* (**2**, 110–112, 1849). Sir Eardley Holland (p. 909) [8] wrote that it appeared in *The British Record* 'for no particular reason'. Clay had reviewed Collins's book in the same volume (pp. 25–28) and Dr. Sims's letter was the first document signed by one of the three Doctors which could be laid before the public. (The second one, the Windsor 'Report', was to be published just over a century later.)

I have not managed to locate the original letter written by Dr. Sims. The present text is that of Collins, who probably owned the letter, being a relative of Dr. Clarke. Lee's and Clay's transcriptions are accurate, except for some slight differences in punctuation and abbreviations, and for the substitution by Clay of 'dispute' for 'differ' regarding the quantity of blood in the cavity of the uterus (§9).

W. S. Playfair included Dr. Sims's letter in one that he sent to the Editor of *The Medical Times and Gazette* on 29 November 1872 ('On the death of the Princess Charlotte of Wales', **2**, 636–637, No. 1171, 7 December 1872). He probably copied Dr. Sims's text from Clay because, like him and unlike Collins and Lee, he wrote 'dispute' instead of 'differ' (§9). Besides introducing some grammatical modifications which do not alter the meaning, Playfair substituted 'soft' for 'short' in the sentence in which Dr. Sims described the Princess's pains (§2) and omitted 'and saw immediately that she must die.' (§8), 'to me' in the phrase 'it does not seem to me quite certain' (§10), and the whole sentence 'As far as I can judge, the labour could not have been better managed.' (§11).

Playfair published the letter again in the second edition of his book *A treatise on the science and practice of midwifery* (Smith, Elder, & Co., London 1878, vol. II, pp. 16–18; the first edition had appeared in 1876), in all subsequent English editions (1880, 1882, 1884, 1886, 1889, 1893, 1898), in the two editions of the Spanish translation (*Tratado teórico y práctico del arte de los partos*, E. Teodoro, Madrid

1880, from the second English edition of 1878, vol. II, pp. 19–21; Bailly-Baillière, Madrid 1890, from the seventh English edition of 1889) and in the French translation (*Traité théorique et pratique de l'art des accouchements*, O. Doin, Paris 1879, pp. 467–469, from the second English edition of 1878). Playfair's letter was also included by G.-J. Witkowski in his book *Les Accouchements à la Cour* (G. Steinheil, Paris, circa 1890, pp. 19–22).

Acknowledgements

I am most grateful to Her Majesty Queen Elizabeth II for her gracious concession to publish the reproduction of the 'Doctors' Report' (Plate III).

Prince Ernst August, Duke of Brunswick-Lüneburg, present Head of the House of Hanover, has graciously allowed me to publish Count Münster's letter (VI); my best thanks to His Royal Highness.

I feel deeply indebted to Richard Page Croft, Esq. (a great-great-grandson of Sir Richard), the owner of 'The New Croft Papers' and of his ancestor's post-mortem portrait (I, II, III, IV and Plates I and II). Without his kind permission to publish them I would not have compiled this paper.

Princess Charlotte's letter to Dr. Baillie (V) and Mrs. Baillie's Notebook (VII) are the property of the Royal College of Surgeons of England. I am very grateful to the President and the Council for kindly allowing me to publish them. E. H. Cornelius, Esq., Librarian of the College, took the trouble of going through all the Baillie papers on my behalf and I appreciate his kind collaboration very much.

My thanks are due to Monsieur le Chevalier Albert de Selliers de Moranville, President, Le Musée de la Dynastie, Brussels, for the reproduction of Princess Charlotte's portrait (Frontispiece) and to The National Trust, Croft Castle, Herefs., for permission to quote the postscript to Sir Thomas Lawrence's letter (Note 1).

I wish to express my most sincere gratitude to the present Lord Croft (another great-great-grandson of Sir Richard) for his continuous very kind encouragement and advice and for all the information he has given me in recent years.

I am grateful to Mrs. Inge Saxon Mills for supplying me with many books, pamphlets and newspapers of the time.

I have to thank many other persons besides those who have helped me with the present paper. I shall not forget them and shall acknowledge my debt to each one in my future book.

And, last but not least, my particularly warm and heartfelt thanks go to Miss Jessica Thompson, former Research Assistant to Prof. Sir David Smithers, for her indefatigable zeal on my behalf. Her collaboration in the transcription of the documents and in bibliographical research has been of fundamental importance.